Blinding Lights

The Glaring Evidences Of The Christian Faith

by

Braxton Hunter

authorHOUSE®

AuthorHouse™
1663 Liberty Drive, Suite 200
Bloomington, IN 47403
www.authorhouse.com
Phone: 1-800-839-8640

© *2008 Braxton Hunter. All rights reserved.*

No part of this book may be reproduced, stored in a retrieval system, or transmitted by any means without the written permission of the author.

First published by AuthorHouse 2/11/2008

ISBN: 978-1-4343-1218-1 (sc)

Printed in the United States of America
Bloomington, Indiana

This book is printed on acid-free paper.

Dedicated to Sarah for being one of God's most blinding lights

Thanks to: Dr. Harold Hunter and Marilyn Hunter for raising me to love the study of God, Chad and Jen, Bob and Betty Scussel, Cornerstone Baptist Church, Son Baptist Church, my closest friends and all who support Trinity Crusades for Christ.

Contents

Forward 1
Introduction 3

SECTION 1
Chapter 1: The Lies Of Naturalism 17
Chapter 2: The Racism of Naturalism 35
Chapter 3: The Fairy Tales Of Naturalism 47
Chapter 4: The Answer to Naturalism 61
Chapter 5: Relativism 77

SECTION 2
Chapter 6: The Prophecies Surrounding His Life . .95
Chapter 7: His Claims, Influence and Sanity 107
Chapter 8: His Death, Burial And Resurrection . .121
Chapter 9: The Trustworthiness Of The Bible 137

SECTION 3
Chapter 10: Why Discredit False Doctrine 155
Chapter 11: Jehovah's Witnesses 167
Chapter 12: Mormonism 187
Chapter 13: Salvation By Works 205
Chapter 14: Understanding Predestination 227
Chapter 15: Examining the Tulip 245

SECTION 4
Chapter 16: The Blinding Lights of a Believer 261
Chapter 17: The Importance Of Fellowship 273
Chapter 18: Knowing The Enemy 285
Chapter 19: Becoming A Blinding Light 295
Chapter 20: True Love 309
Chapter 21: Three Tools For The Journey 321

Chapter 22: Communicating With God 335
Appendix A: Summary of Apologetics for the Existence of the Christian God. 345
Appendix B: Alternate Introduction 353
Appendix C: The Three Wise Men 367
Appendix D: The Trinity-Not A Deal Breaker . . .379

Forward

Without a doubt apologetics is something of a lost art. In the past, Theology was known to be composed of Dogmatics, Ethics, and . . . Apologetics.
Presently, a scan of catalogs from seminaries worldwide will scarcely reveal this essential apologetic portion of the theological craft. But we must know not only what we believe, but why. Apologetics is precisely this: an attempt to lay out, in a rationally compelling, consistent, coherent, and comprehensive way, the 'faith once delivered to the saints.' In our day and age of pluralism, multiculturalism, postmodernism, and skepticism, the Truth still stands and the evidence must be told: Jesus Christ, crucified, dead, buried, risen again, and appearing to over 500 witnesses at once. Jesus himself gave 'many convincing proofs' of his resurrection and in turn his deity. We must continue to lay forth this evidence that the world may know- and in turn, be turned upside down!
Edward N. Martin, Ph.D.

Professor of Philosophy and Theology
Associate Chairman of Philosophy and Theology
Liberty University

Introduction

There is no such thing as darkness. It simply doesn't exist. Skeptics in our time often ask believers, "If God exists, why is there so much darkness in the world?" By this they mean evil. How could a loving God allow so much evil to exist? This seems like a fair question. However, the problem is that if there are no such things as darkness or evil, they cannot exist of themselves. Think about it. Do scientists measure darkness or light? We can discuss how bright a room may be. In fact, we may logically talk about the brightness of the sun or that of a distant star. The inevitable conclusion is that a place only gets darker since less and less light is present. Once there is absolutely no light present at all, the object becomes completely dark and will, quite obviously, never get darker than that. Darkness only exists as the absence of light. In the same way, evil only exists as the absence of good. This book is focused on shining a light into the dark corners of Christianity that have been ignored for so long. To do this, you need to understand a couple of things.

If you are no stranger to the subject at hand, an alternate introduction of greater detail is contained in Appendix B.

For a long time I have been told by Christian leaders whom I respect that belief in God is something that must be established purely on the credibility of faith without regard to worldly evidences. I accepted this until one day as I studied the Bible I saw a verse that simply did not fit into that framework. The verse I read was 1 Peter 3:15 which demands, ***"But sanctify the Lord God in your hearts: and be ready always to give an answer to every man that asketh you a reason of the hope that is in you with meekness and fear."*** Suddenly, taking it all on faith did not make sense. God had just demanded through Peter that I have evidence for my faith and that I share it with anyone interested. Wait a minute! Evidence? Everybody knows there is no real hard evidence that God exists. There certainly isn't any evidence that Jesus is God. Or is there? If so, why have I never heard a preacher talk about it? After a few days of dizzying confusion it occurred to me that if God could be discovered with testable criterion the means for finding him would be logic. Logic is the key! God has revealed himself to us. Like he did with Moses while his face was half buried in the mountainside, God has passed our way and for a moment shown himself.

There are two ways in which God has been revealed. The first way has to do with the universe around us and is referred to as *general revelation.* God's existence, personality and many of his desires are discoverable by observing the creation around us. The second and more obvious way God may have revealed himself is through what is known as *special revelation.* This refers to written or spoken revelation from God such as the Bible. Whether or not you believe the Bible is the Word of God is not necessary at this point. Instead, you simply need to be aware of this teaching. Understanding these two ways that God has revealed himself to mankind is paramount if you are going to get anything out of this book. The first half will deal with general revelation (what we can know about God from observing the universe). The second half of this book will deal with special revelation (what the Bible specifically says about God). Each argument will build on the last and no argument (including whether or not the Bible is God's Word) will be based on bad evidence. Because of this, there are four sections to this book that will build on each other. Section one will argue the fallacies of naturalism and the reasons why science and philosophy prove the existence of God beyond a reasonable doubt. The next section will address the man named Jesus and why he should or should not be considered the one true God. Section three will answer the question, "Which version of Jesus is the right one?" Cults, false doctrines and varying beliefs about Jesus will be discussed and in the final section you will be challenged to make a decision.

This book is only a glimmer, a spark, but within its pages you will find a path to light. If you are a skeptic, the path will lead you into the light and as you travel on the quest the darkness will fade around you. I am confident of this. For present believers the path will lead you to surety and understanding of the light with which you are already familiar. Whatever your situation may be, each page is part of a plan for igniting your life and the world around you. It is an exciting path and an excellent plan. You should be enthusiastic about the journey. One word of caution must be submitted. Remember, there is no darkness! How dim your existence is depends on how far you are from that which is bright. You have the power to light up the evening sky by observing and ultimately becoming the glaring evidence of God and his Son. Those evidences are blinding lights!

Important Terms

If it is the hope of this endeavor to discover the reality of a higher power, namely the divine person of Jesus Christ, several presuppositions must be made. It must first be established whether or not the universe was designed by some sort of intelligence. Dismissing this possibility results in the irrelevance of any dialogue involving the spiritual realm. No designer means no God. No God means only naturalism. Only naturalism means nothing spiritual exists, and if this is the case it is futile to discuss the divinity of Jesus or anyone else. Because of this, it is needful to establish the existence of a designer before moving on to the possibility that Jesus Christ embodies within himself all the attributes that are necessary to be identified as God. For this, we must understand some of the terms that have been used in the past regarding the search for a creator.

Until the last two centuries, there was little debate about the existence of a designer. Were there atheists? Absolutely. Did naturalism exist? Of course it did. However, the idea that all biological developments came to exist by way of purely natural processes (evolution) had not been popularized. Thus, when it was, an enthusiasm for abandoning religion resulted. But what specifically was believed prior to the popularization of naturalism?

Creationism

"Creationism" was long accepted as a valid scientific philosophy. Simply put, creationism claims that what the Bible says in the first eleven chapters of Genesis is to be taken as the literal story of the beginning of the universe. Indeed, many of the educational establishments that exist today as esteemed purveyors of modern evolutionary and naturalistic thought were begun by academics who believed almost exclusively in creationism.

In recent years, creationists have become more aggressive in their stance against all things naturalistic. The abandonment of any metaphoric, symbolic or figurative interpretation of the book of Genesis has gained them vast acceptance among conservative Christians today. After all, how could a born again Christian fault the efforts of a man who seeks to establish the historical reliability of the Bible? Unfortunately, there is one great downfall to the philosophy of creationism.

While listening to the arguments of many creationists, a trend seems to surface. That trend is a dependence upon special revelation (i. e. the Bible) alone. As mentioned in the introduction, if God exists, he has given man two distinctive methods for discovering him which are general revelation (what is observable in the universe) and special revelation (God's direct communication by way of scripture.) You might ask, "What's wrong with appealing only to the Bible?" Nothing! If one can be persuaded to believe by scripture alone, then special revelation is all that is required. Unfortunately, the modern culture is skeptical. Creationism's primary weakness is that it fails to address the scientific arguments of the day.

The previous statement would not be acceptable to creationists, but by and large it is the case. While some creationists attempt to debunk the flaws in evolution and answer their arguments, in most (not all) cases it becomes difficult to discern who is the subject of the creationist's argument; liberal Christians who do not accept the literal Bible or evolutionists. Sadly, the unbalanced approach to the matter focuses more on special revelation and less on general revelation thereby succeeding in exciting the passions of those who are already believers, but seldom convincing a naturalist. Conversely, there is a group of apologists who argue from the other extreme.

Intelligent Design

"Intelligent Design" (ID) has become popular in recent years. In response to the arguable failure of the creationist, ID advocates seek to argue only for general revelation (what is revealed in the universe about a designer). Strengthening the Christian apologetic cause, this movement answers successfully many of the arguments upheld by the naturalist. Focusing on the great evidences in general revelation for a designer, ID adherents demand honesty and confession from naturalists about the false aspects of their arguments. Still, the ID movement is flawed as well.

Intelligent Design falls short of excellence for the same reason as creationism. It is unbalanced. Remember, the necessary line that must be walked. General revelation and special revelation must both be kept in mind. The ID advocates miss the mark by arguing exclusively for general revelation. It is, in their opinion, the strength of their argument. Unfortunately, general revelation can only take us so far. By the means upheld herein, it can be successfully argued that there is a designer, but this does not help one to discover the identity of that designer. For this reason, general revelation should always be followed by its counterpart, special revelation.

Intelligent Design and Creationism in their place

Despite how it may seem, I am not arguing for a dismissal of either of these philosophies. It is my contention that they each have their place in the apologetic debate. Pearls of great price exist within each of these circles. So what are the great treasures to be gleaned?

A moderate view of creationism is needful among Christians today. If there is a God and he came to earth in the form of the man Jesus, Christians must have a basic understanding of what they believe about him and his role in the origin of life on and above earth. The weakness of creationism for the apologetic debate is its strength for Christendom. Once someone has accepted the premise that general revelation indicates a creator, they may proceed to special revelation with confidence. In this regard, the creationist is of great value for his ability to firm up the faith of those who have already trusted in Christ. From a distance, intelligent design has its role as well.

ID's greatest arena is the educational and scientific community. To the Christian readers I must say, let's be realistic. We no longer live in a world that accepts biblical creation as a valid scientific theory. However, repackaged in the form of ID, the biblical worldview is a valid scientific theory held by many biologists today. Unfortunately, so many believers today have clung to the creationists' arguments so exclusively that they have thrown out the proverbial baby with the bath water. What is wrong with pressing the ID argument in the classroom as a valid, non-religious argument, devoid as it may be of Jesus? At least then we would have gained some ground. You might say, "What good does it do us to convince them that there is a God if they never hear of Jesus?"

Often times my ministry, "Trinity Crusades for Christ," has been invited to make presentations at area high schools and middle schools around the country. The only stipulation is that nothing religious is ever mentioned. Because of this, an inspirational, albeit secular, talk is given on the subject of teenage suicide. Remember, nothing about God can be said. Yet, often students are so moved by the experience that when their friends invite them to a Christian meeting that night at a local church, the student is pleased to attend. At this point, the gospel may be shared without apology. Many have converted to Christianity and benefited immeasurably by this system.

Is there any harm in attempting a similar endeavor with ID? Why can we not promote it as a valid non-religious scientific theory on par with evolution so that students can receive a non-biased education? Like the student who hears a presentation on teen-suicide, the one who understands that there is some force behind the creation of all life will begin a search at which time intelligent design can pass the baton to creationism.

Understanding all of this, you may regard the relevant sections of this book as a work of what I call "Theistic ID," a balanced view of intelligent design and creationism. The arguments shall be made from an ID standpoint, but followed with a theistic understanding of the implications.

SECTION 1

In order that the Christian faith may be true, it must first be established that there is a spiritual realm as well as a Creator. If this is not true, there is no sense in pursuing a religious faith in anything or anyone. Consequently, section one is presented first that we may establish with reasonable certainty that there is a Creator and that this Creator reveals himself through general revelation in nature. For this we need not appeal to the Bible or any other documents claiming to be special revelation from God. So blinding are these lights that they are obvious even without the Bible. God exists! Spirituality is real! Truth is absolute!

Chapter 1: The Lies Of Naturalism

During the writing of this book I have seen the beauty of God. I have shouted praises to the creator with villagers deep in the jungles of the Philippines under a canopy of stars, and baptized new converts in the China Sea. I have received communion with Bahamians on the majestic islands of the Caribbean and buried my feet in the warm white beaches of Mexico. Observing God's people in Israel it occurred to me that God could engineer a nation with the same detail as he could galaxies, and when I saw St. Peter's Basilica in Italy I knew that he had passed on that fascination with creativity to mankind.

Such beauty may be enough to convince many of the reality and personality of God. Those with that degree of spiritual insight have my respect. They are able to see beyond the mechanics of the faith and ascertain a pure trust in what God has said. However, some of us want to see the solid, tangible evidence that what we are trusting is real. Crude as this may sound it is not only necessary but endorsed by scripture. Unfortunately, many skeptics today have demanded that looking at the evidence from nature there is no reason to believe in God, nor a spiritual realm. One of the primary reasons for this is the work that has been going on for decades regarding biological evolution.

When you step back from the numbers and data, examining it with your common sense, evolution is revealed as one of the most baseless ideas ever conceived by man. This is not to say that the philosophy is not well thought out. Nor may we claim that it does not have its evidences. However, it is my contention that there are more holes in evolutionary thought than there are in that of "Theistic ID." Both are valid theories, but the difference is simple. Where the "Theistic ID" advocate has unanswered questions, he appeals to proven, testable scripture for an answer, while the evolutionist (without a holy manuscript) often develops deceptive arguments to propagate his theory. He lies.

When my father was the pastor of a prominent church in Florida, a very pompous looking man came through the doors of the building one day. As my father was standing there greeting congregants, he said to this man, "May I help you find a Sunday school class?" The man, not knowing who my father was, replied, "No sir, I know my way around. The pastor, Dr. Hunter, and I go way back." My father was Dr. Hunter and replied, "Really?" He said, "Yes, I go golfing with Dr. Hunter every week." My father didn't even own a set of golf clubs. The man continued, "What's more, Dr. Hunter takes me out on his boat every Saturday." My father didn't even know that he owned a boat; this was a pretty good day for him. The man went in, sat down and had a look of absolute horror on his face when he saw that the real Dr. Hunter stood to preach.

Lies are tricky things. They must be developed thoughtfully and with great care. Because of the nature of untruth, logic has the ability to expose a lie for what it is.

In this chapter, to the best of my ability I will share with you some of the lies that have been used by evolutionists for years and then we will close by talking about some of the most recent deceptions.

Charles Darwin knew of one fatal flaw in his theory of the origin of species. That flaw was simple. If species developed because of random variations over billions of years, there would have to be examples found in fossils or skeletal structures that represented a missing link that bridged the gap between species. For example, it has long been preached by the evolutionist that the dinosaurs evolved into birds. I know that if you have not studied this it may sound silly, but that is what they believe. In fact, this myth has never been more popular than since the Steven Spielberg film, "Jurassic Park," hit theaters in the mid-nineties. But if that is true, there must be a middle ground. There would have to be a missing link between the dinosaurs and the birds. There must somewhere be a fossil or a skeletal structure of a dinosaur with wings. Darwin knew that this sort of thing was a problem. He and other evolutionists passed it off by saying, "Well, we don't know where these missing links are, but we have faith that they'll be discovered in the near future." The problem is, they never were discovered.

The longer that time went by without a missing link, the less evolution was respected and, as a theory, began to die. So what was the one thing that evolutionists could do to keep the theory going and their grant money coming? They could lie. So they did. They said they had found the missing link.

A recent example took place several years ago. National Geographic published an article in which they claimed the skeletal remains of a dinosaur with feathers had been found, supposedly proving evolution by locating one of many needed "missing links." The scientific world was thrilled. At least they were thrilled until, with closer observation, the findings were determined to be a hoax. After the findings were cast, National Geographic issued this statement:

" WASHINGTON—Based on the best scientific information available at press time, NATIONAL GEOGRAPHIC reported on the *Archaeoraptor* fossil in the November issue of the magazine. Only after the magazine had been published did NATIONAL GEOGRAPHIC learn about the possibility that the fossil might be a composite. If it is a composite, it initially escaped detection by a team of scientists that included top experts on bird origins. We immediately began an investigation into the matter and took the earliest possible opportunity to publish a disclosure of the new information in NATIONAL GEOGRAPHIC magazine (March 2000). We were obviously disappointed to hear that *Archaeoraptor* might be a composite and are committed to getting to the bottom of the mystery of this fossil. The magazine will report the findings to its readers. NATIONAL GEOGRAPHIC is currently in negotiations with scientists in China and the U.S. to get the fossils together for an independent review. This is the only way to determine conclusively if *Archaeoraptor* is a composite. We also funded the original CT scanning work on the fossil and hope to see the published analysis in a peer-reviewed journal soon. Regardless of

Archaeoraptor, most paleontologists have been convinced for some time that birds emerged from dinosaurs. This is based on a wealth of evidence unrelated to any of the current fossils from China.

February 3, 2000"

What does this statement mean? It means after shoddy journalism and unsure reporting, National Geographic discovered their find to be a farce; but, like Darwin, they had enough faith to believe that one day the evidence would be there. Lies and misplaced ambitions were the motors that kept this story alive for so long. Do you know what could have shown us from the start that this was a lie? We could have stepped back and used common sense. Because of this silly story and the obvious fiction of Steven Spielberg's movie, when I want you to think about something with common sense in the remainder of this book, I will refer to it as "Jurassic Park sense."

But these lies go back further than that. They needed missing links for cave men too. You know about cave men. They are supposedly the missing link between men and monkeys. In fact, about the time of the Scopes trial that some believe disproved biblical creation, there was a skeletal structure of a "cave man" known as Piltdown man. He was hailed as the evidence for evolution. In fact, newspapers and college professors called it absolute proof. This "evidence" was used in a trial to prove creation wrong. The problem is that a few years after the Scopes trial, Piltdown man was proven to be a fraud. Consider the following medical examination:

"The original Piltdown teeth were produced and examined by three scientists. The evidence it was a fake could be seen immediately. The first and second molars were worn to the same degree; the inner margins of the lower teeth were more worn than the outer -- the 'wear' was the wrong way round; the edges of the teeth were sharp and unbeveled; the exposed areas of dentine were free of shallow cavities and flush with the surrounding enamel; the biting surface of the two molars did not form a uniform surface, the planes were out of alignment. That the teeth might have been misplaced after the death of Piltdown man was considered but an X-ray showed the lower contact surfaces of the roots were correctly positioned. This X-ray also revealed that contrary to the 1916 radiograph the roots were unnaturally similar in length and disposition. The molar surfaces were examined under a microscope. They were scarred by criss-cross scratches suggesting the use of an abrasive. 'The evidences of artificial abrasion immediately sprang to the eye' wrote Le Gros Clark. 'Indeed so obvious did they [the scratches] seem it may well be asked -- how was it that they had escaped notice before?' He answered his question with a beautiful simplicity. 'They had never been looked for...nobody previously had examined the Piltdown jaw with the idea of a possible forgery in mind, a deliberate fabrication.'"[1]

Next they brought up Neanderthal man. Oh, he is surely proof of evolution because he has apelike features. Actually, a French paleontologist studied him and found that he suffered from diseases that made his bones malformed, but since the evolutionists had decided that Piltdown man must be an ape-man they said, "So is Neanderthal man." Really he was just a guy with bad arthritis. In an article published in Creation magazine Don Batten writes:

"There is a long list of defunct 'ape-men'. Neanderthal man heads the list. Evolutionists hailed remains found in 1856 as man's ancestor, but now it is admitted that the supposedly stooped posture was due to disease, and Neanderthal is really just a variant of the human kind."[2]

In fact even in Lebanon, Tennessee, a small town outside of Nashville, there is a man whose greatest claim in life is that he says he has the head of a caveman. However, when people approach him from respectable schools to examine the skull he refuses them and says that it wouldn't be respectful to the caveman. What he is really saying is, "I'm lying; please don't expose me."

Yet, in spite of all of this, we should really be angered that in text books today we still have that picture of an ape turning more and more into a man and grunting his way up to becoming a man, based solely on findings like Piltdown man and Neanderthal man. Evolution is a religion based on lies.

Why do they make up such absurd stories? That is what you do when there is a deficit of evidence. For a century and a half, evolutionists have scoured the globe and used every means imaginable to uncover some fossil record of transitional (missing link) species. In all of that time there is still no real reason to accept the teachings of evolution. Leading geologist, David Raup, at the Field Museum of Natural History explains:

> ". . . we are now about 120 years after Darwin and the knowledge of the fossil record has been greatly expanded. We now have a quarter of a million fossil species but the situation hasn't changed much. The record of evolution is still surprisingly jerky and, ironically, we have even fewer examples of evolutionary transitions than we had in Darwin's time. By this I mean that some of the classic cases of Darwinian change in the fossil record, such as the evolution of

the horse in North America, have had to be discarded or modified as a result of more detailed information – what appeared to be a nice simple progression when relatively few data were available now appears to be much more complex and much less gradualistic."[3]

If Americans weren't dumbed down by certain government institutions, people would have Jurassic park sense and know that Darwinian evolution is fiction.

I remember telling my teacher a lie when I was in second grade. I had sneaked out of my classroom by telling my teacher that I was leaving early that day to go to a nearby city because my mother wanted to do some shopping, and I had to go with her. I even made it sound like I was upset that I had to leave school. It was a pretty elaborate lie for someone my age. And then I sneaked all through the school and dodged teachers all day. It felt like mission impossible. I was even seen a couple of times, but I quickly disappeared into the sea of lockers and students. I did all of this, but made one mistake. I ended up right outside of my father's office, the president of the school, and he saw me. Little did I know that my teacher had already called him. She saw right through my well- planned lie, and I got the worst spanking of my life. My father had a belt that was so big I am convinced that they used all the leather from the cow.

Now I may have been in second grade, but I had a pretty good lie. However, they saw right through it. Tell me why some of the smartest people in the world can see through lies that are planned out so well, but they wholeheartedly believe the senseless and baseless claims of the evolutionist. Where is our Jurassic park sense? Startling as it is, while man's understanding of the universe deepens, so do the lies needed to explain away God.

Do you remember being taught that the appendix was left over from evolution and that it doesn't have a function? Many parts of the human body classified as no longer useful are labeled vestigial organs and the evolutionists say there are 180 of them. Would you like to have them all removed?

Shocking to the disciples of evolution, it has now been discovered that the appendix has all sorts of uses. Still, there are some structures in your body that are useless leftovers. There are some structures that were used when you were a fetus being born that have no use today, but that is not evolution.

Some say we are evolving because we lose our wisdom teeth. Actually, modern children are maturing more quickly, and there is no room for those teeth. Evolution says you are gaining something and getting better, but losing wisdom teeth is not gaining information; it is losing information. It's like the orthopedic surgeon who recently said, "Man's tail bone looks surprisingly like it was once longer and formed a proper tail. This must be evolution at work." Actually if man had never had a tail and grew one today that was useful somehow then you might have evidence for evolution, but if you lose a tail you have lost information and are getting worse.

I remember learning to ride a bicycle very well. For years all I had known was a tiny black bike with training wheels. I wanted to ride a man's bike. Mr. Nelson who was our next-door neighbor promised that he had a man's bike that he would teach me to ride whenever I was ready. To be honest I was pretty content with my training wheels. Everything changed one day at school when Billy came in and announced that he no longer used training wheels and had graduated to a man's bike. That day at precisely 3:31pm I knocked on Mr. Nelson's door and said, "I'm ready to ride a man's bike." You wouldn't believe what a man's bike looked like. It was technically a woman's bike and if that wasn't bad enough it was pink. I never figured out what Amazon woman rode that pink monstrosity, the seat came up to my chest. Still, the time came when Mr. Nelson let go of that bike and I was off. Everything was going fine until I noticed a large turtle making his way across the street in front of me. Today I would have plowed on through, but things are different when you're younger and don't have as many kills on your record. At this moment and not before, I realized that I never learned how to brake. My little bike had a brake in the pedal, but this one didn't. I had noticed the strangely shaped metal object on the handlebars but paid it no attention. Only later would I find out that the strange metal object would have solved everything. Unfortunately, I ended up face down in the ditch promising never to ride again.

This is the problem with scientists claiming that anomalies in the body have no function. As has occurred time and again, researchers will discover all sorts of uses for what have been termed vestigial organs and as they're lying humiliated in the ditch of intellectual ignorance, ridiculed for their naivety, they will wonder why didn't I give that strange thing a second look.

When people say an organ is useless and has no function, they have made an arrogant assumption. Just because you can't see a function doesn't mean that an organ doesn't have a function; it just means you don't know what the function is. People once thought that tonsils had no function. Now we know they do. The latest lie is a little more clever. Some say the panda bear has a thumb that is useless and ill- designed. The truth is the panda bear has a thumb that is ideal for collecting the kinds of foods he eats. Scientists today gladly claim that certain things don't have a use when the reality is their ignorance and *a prior* disposition to a creator causes them to be blinded. The truth is they just have no idea what the purposes of these creations are.

So you may ask the question, "Why would scientists propagate an idea that they know to be false? And why would so many intelligent people push aside their Jurassic park sense and believe this fiction to be reality?" Here is why.

If evolution is true, then man is one step closer to proving that there is no such thing as God. If man can prove that there is no God, he is one step closer to proving that there is no moral code. If man can prove that there is no moral code, then he can live however he wants. There would be no right or wrong and he could do as he pleased.

Evolutionary scientists have even more reason for clinging to the dying faith of evolution. Anyone who believes in creation is thought to be ignorant and religious, while those who make headway in the field of evolutionary biology are praised, promoted and receive awards. To believe anything else would be career suicide for a scientist today. Now don't misunderstand, there are good scientists, professors and teachers who have Jurassic park sense and know the truth. But they are mocked and scoffed at by their contemporaries even though the majority of the evidence points to theism beyond a reasonable doubt.

Yet, as I said earlier, the primary reason people gladly accept atheistic evolution is because it means they can be their own gods and live however they choose. Children are also being raped of their Jurassic Park sense. If you ask a child how the world got started, most of them who are not even churched will tell you that it was God. But by the time they get to high school, the world has found a way to feed them lies as well.

I have in my office a copy of the textbook, *Biology: Principles and Explorations* by Holt, Rinehart and Winston.[4] For the most part, this book does a good job of trying to stay neutral, even though on August 14, 2001, a Georgia teen named Rebecca Moeller was so enraged by its teaching that she sued the school system over this same book.

On page 288 of the book in Chapter 13 it, explains the "Haekel experiment" in which the embryos of several different animals were shown to come from one common ancestor that had gill slits proving that evolution must be true. Are you aware that in 1860 this was admittedly faked by its creator? Yet it is taught in our public school system today as a good scientific theory even though it was proven false.

Is this not enough to show that evolution is a religion based on lies? On page 254 of the book, there is a figure of the "Miller-Urey" experiment in which Miller creates an atmosphere in a system of tubes that is supposed to be like the atmosphere in the early earth. By shooting electricity through it, he supposedly brought organic life from inorganic substances. The problem, as even the book points out, is that his understanding of the early atmosphere is now labeled as false. Even so, this experiment is placed in our textbooks as a good scientific evidence of evolution. The real problem with this is that even if Miller had brought life from these materials, it is more of a proof of creation than evolution because he was an intelligent person creating life instead of leaving it to happen by random variation.

These are at least two examples of things in the textbook that our kids take home, and they are proven lies. They are not theories, they are not probabilities; they are lies. Even evolutionists no longer accept them, but they are in our textbooks.

Everything we have discussed so far has been taught for years, but now there is a new lie. In recent years, it has become clear for reasons that have and will be discussed in following chapters that species of life do not evolve into other species although they do change within themselves. Certain types of plant life have experienced micro-evolution (simple changes within their own species). This happens, but it is not evolution. The plant did not change into a dog, but this micro-change has been labeled speciation and held up as proof of evolution. But the evolutionist knows that this is not at all the same as what they are asserting. Evolution is not a tenable belief.

I hope that you will look at these facts with the knowledge and understanding of an educated person and see it for what it is. Then, step back and look at the agenda of a manufactured religion that has a history of perpetually lying. I understand that the presence of liars within the community of biological evolution is not a good enough reason for dismissing the philosophy as a whole. However, conclusive reasons for that will be seen in following chapters. Rather ask yourself a question. What should you believe? Should you believe a faith that changes every year, or a faith that has never changed?

[1] Millar, Ronald. *The Piltdown Men*. St. Martin's Press.

[2] Batten, Don. First published: *Creation* 18(3):42–45 June 1996.

[3] Raup, David M. *Conflicts between Darwin and Paleontology*. Bulletin, Field Museum of Natural History, Janiary 1979, pp. 23.

[4] Holt, Rinehart and Winston, Inc. *Biology: Principles and Explorations* 1998.

Chapter 2: The Racism of Naturalism

It is my intent through this chapter to make it clear to all readers that evolution is a racist religion and must be shown as such. Please understand that I am not arguing that this alone is a good enough reason to dismiss the hypothesis, nor am I saying that all evolutionists are racist. Rather, by showing the harm that has been done by this philosophy I hope you will be compelled to consider closely whether it is a beneficial teaching. Consider the actions and views of early evolutionists regarding the Australian aborigines:

"A death bed memoir from Korah Wills, who became mayor of Bowen, Queensland, in 1866, graphically describes how he killed and dismembered a local tribesman in 1865 to provide a scientific specimen."[1]

"Edward Ramsey, curator of the Australian Museum in Sydney (1874-1894) published a museum booklet that appeared to describe Aborigines as 'Australian animals.' It also gave instructions on how to rob graves and plug bullet wounds in freshly killed 'specimens.' He complained in the 1880s that a Queensland law to stop slaughtering Aborigines was affecting his supply."[1]

"Amalie Dietrich, a German evolutionist (nicknamed the 'Angel of Black Death'), came to Australia and asked that Aborigines be shot for specimens so their skin could be stuffed and mounted. 'Although evicted from at least one property, she shortly returned home with her specimens.'" [1]

"A new South Wales missionary was a horrified witness to the slaughter by mounted police of a group of Aboriginal men, women and children. Forty-five heads were then boiled down and the best 10 skulls were packed off for overseas." [1]

This is clearly a racist religion. As we discuss this and seek out the real answer behind the kaleidoscope of diversity in the world today, I want you to keep in mind that the same people who are propelling the idea of racist evolution are often the ones who claim that we ought to be tolerant of others, respect everyone despite who they are, create a socialist government because everyone deserves equal pay, and forget all our differences.

That should be difficult for some so-called races to do. Are you aware that at the time Darwinian evolution was at its height, there were charts circling in scientific communities on which were drawn the outline of the skulls of every race of people? Based on the normality of shape, scientists decided that the white man was clearly capable of the most intelligent thought while Asian, Hispanic and almost every other people-group was placed significantly lower, and black people were placed right above the apes as far as intelligence is concerned.

The worst part about it is that this does not really bother most of us-- at least not those of us who are white. Christians might say, "Well, that shouldn't be," or, "That's wrong," but even in the church today there is a racist overtone that hangs in the air because Darwinian evolution has been hammered into our minds through the culture for years and years. As the result, we think this way whether we realize it or not. In fact, I have had some Christians admit to me that they feel that other races are not quiet capable of the same mental processes that they are.

When I was pastoring in Jacksonville, Florida, the church was nestled in a predominately black area. Naturally, I attempted to attract our neighbors to join our church when they would come. Rather than being delighted at our new brothers and sisters in Christ, some of the elderly members went to them in private and said, "We're glad you want to praise the Lord, but there is a nice black church down the road for you." One of our men came to me and said, "What are you doing bringing all this trash in here?" I was so enraged by this that I found a black minister in the community who was without a church at the time and asked him to come on staff with us and be a kind of associate pastor. He sat on stage with me every time I preached and often preached in my absence. Those cruel church members had to stare at God's man who happened to be a different skin tone every Sunday, elevated behind the pulpit high above the crowd.

You might say, "Well, if evolution is true then we just have to accept it." I agree, but there is a much more logical explanation for how the races came about that fits better with what we see in the world and happens to line up with biblical creation.

Are you aware that there are groups of people around the world who have stories handed down from before they ever met a Christian that were almost identical to those stories of creation that are in the Bible. Woman was made while man was asleep, and there was a boat and a great flood and man survived on the boat and had three sons on a mountain, and God put a rainbow in the sky. Also, there was a man who had a tree with wonderful nectar in it and he was warned not to eat of that tree, but he did and death came into the world. Have you heard stories like those? They sound like Genesis, don't they? They are a little different, but ultimately undeniably the same. Are you aware that those same kinds of stories are heard from around the world? The Hawaiians, the Eskimos, American Indians and the Babylonians all had stories like those. It seems clear that the reason that they have stories in their culture so similar to the Bible is because they have been handed down from generation to generation. Though they have changed a little, the record is basically biblical. All these peoples do go back to Noah and even Adam. Every human in the world today goes all the way back to Adam and Eve.

Shockingly, even though we have the same parents, come from the same people and are all relatives, we still have racist attitudes even in the church. If I ask the average person how many races there are in the world, they might answer "Oh, eight, ten or twelve," but modern biology has proven that no two people anywhere on planet earth differ by more than one percent genetically. There is only one race of people.

Unfortunately, there are atheists in the world today leading the way in ending racism when actually the church ought to be on the forefront of such a battle. We are all descendants of one man, Adam. There is only one race, biologically; we are the same. The Bible explains all of this. What should bother us is that there are Bible colleges telling students that God actually made different races of men all over the world, and that is why we have different characteristics.

The task that lies before us now is to explain with clarity why it is that people in different parts of the world have different characteristics and different traits since it can truly be said that we all came from two original parents. This is not an easy question to answer.

What evolutionists believed in the time of Darwin was simple. They felt that because there are micro-evolutionary changes in certain kinds of animals that macro-evolution is a reality. Darwin understood that when you see those changes, you are seeing evidence that given enough time, one species is going to change into another.

Do you remember high school biology? You get one set of genes from your mother, one from your father and then fertilization takes places. Individuals are the result, and the process is repeated. Do you know how many atoms are in the known universe? There are ten to the 80th power. That's a ten followed by 80 zeros. But do you know how many children a couple could have before getting two that are exactly the same-- a one followed by two-thousand and seventeen zeroes, and God bless the parents that have that many in order to prove that calculation. That's an incredible amount of variability and God built that variability into our genes, cat genes, dog genes and so on. You have all these millions of genes bouncing around, and you get one set from the mother and one from the father, but the dogs still just have dog genes and the cats just have cat genes and the humans just have human genes.

You say, "Well, I can understand that but how do you get these different kinds like black bears and brown bears, grizzly bears and polar bears?" Ok, if you believe the story of Noah's ark is true, how many bears were on the ark? The answer is two. They got off the ark and they started reproducing, and by that time there was a different world. The bears started traveling and inhabiting different areas. Think about this, if you have bears that have genes for short hair and some with genes for long hair and they move up to a colder climate, what is going to happen? The bears with the genes for shorter hair are going to die out and the bears with the genes for long hair are going to thrive; so now a community of all long haired bears has been created and all they will have from then on is long hair. The same is true of color and size. Bears change that way due to natural selection, but that is not evolution. It produces different kinds of bears, but not different animals out of bears. Have you ever seen a bear turn into a kitten? That is not going to happen.

It is actually the opposite of evolution because evolution says that new information is coming in, but when short-haired bears die out and that gene is gone, you've had loss of information and that is the opposite of evolution. Still, this is misrepresented in the classroom today.

Do you know what is being taught in textbooks? The idea that flies build up a resistance to pesticides is commonly taught. Truthfully, they don't build up resistance to pesticides. The same thing happens that I just described with the bear. In every study of insect resistance that has been recorded, the resistant gene was already there. When they were sprayed with the pesticide, the researcher knocked out the non-resistant ones and the ones that were resistant lived and bred more resistance. That's not new information. As some have said, they didn't develop a resistance to hammers or flyswatters. The same is true with viruses and bacteria.

All the bears we have today could come from one male and one female bear. And when people scoff at you about Noah's ark and say, "Awe, how could he get all those animals on the ark?" You should respond by saying, "How many did he really need?" He didn't need several different kinds of bears; he just needed two bears. He didn't need several different kinds of dogs; he needed two dogs.

When Darwin published his book in 1859 on the origin of species, people didn't realize that evolution is a racist philosophy. It teaches that some cultures are closer to the apelike creatures of the past. Now there were racist views before Darwin and there always will be, but evolution promoted it like no other philosophy had. Let me share with you some of the influences of evolution on our thinking here in America.

In America in 1904 at the world's fair in St. Louis, an explorer brought a pigmy from the Congo back to America and put him on display to contrast his primitive culture with advanced technology. When the world's fair ended, there was a deal made with the Bronx Zoo and the pigmy was put in the zoo in a monkey cage with an orangutan, all in the name of evolution. Consider what Carl Sifakis wrote about this pigmy:

> "The man who was put on display in a zoo was brought from the Belgian Congo in 1904 by noted African explorer Samuel Verner. The man, a pygmy named Ota Benga (or 'Bi', which meant 'friend' in his language), was soon 'presented by Verner to the Bronx Zoo director, William Hornaday."[2]

Listen, friends, if it were not for evolution, this idea would never have gained popularity. Would racism have existed? Yes, but would it be as big a problem as it is today? Absolutely not! Evolution is a racist philosophy and must be seen that way. This fact alone should be enough for us to stop teaching it in school.

Still, the question of characteristics has not been thoroughly exhausted. Earlier it was explained that many bears change features over the course of several generations because the ones that survive are the ones that are most adequate for their surroundings. Once again, this is not implicit of evolution, but is simply micro-evolution within a kind. It has been well established that the difference between any two people on the planet is substantially less than .1% genetically speaking. Jonathan Marks, a biological anthropologist at the University of North Carolina at Charlotte claims:

> "Biologists estimate that any two people on earth share 999 out of every 1,000 DNA bases, the 'letters' of the genetic code. Within the human population, all genetic variations—the inheritable differences in our physical appearance, health, and personality—add up to just 0.1 percent of about 3 billion bases."

Educated and logical people today must put aside the asinine idea that there are different "races" in the world today. God created one people. We are the human race. The differences that are recognizable to us are primarily aesthetic variations due to nonevolutionary natural selection. It should also be stated that the implication of this is that there is no difference in the mental capacity within the races. Outside of agreed upon mental disorders that can occur within any group of people and cultural differences which may prohibit development, we are all the same.

Before leaving the subject of race it should be explained that the tower of Babel is described biblically as an event at which God confused the languages of the people but not their physical features. You might ask, "If that is true, then how did all the colors and facial features and differences arise that we see today?" They arose in the same way the differences occurred in those bears. People naturally adapted to their surroundings, but that's not evolution. You might say, "But what about the colors?" What color were Adam and Eve? If Adam and Eve had an olive complexion that was not very dark and not very light, from them could be born both light skinned children or dark skinned children. This is a documented medical truth. I believe that was the case, and it is certainly a lot easier to believe than the racist religion of evolution.

When I was pastoring in Jacksonville, Florida, we had a special event at our church. We called it African American day. We invited many of our African American friends to come and be a part of the festivities at our church during the morning services. We had two prominent African American singers come and I tried to preach with the enthusiasm of an African American preacher. Maybe there is one genetic advancement. They have a natural ability to preach like nobody else. We had many African American and white people convert that day. Several African Americans joined our church. Sadly, there were some of our older members who didn't like this, but I really didn't care what they thought. These were God's children, no different spiritually or genetically from the rest of us and the church needs to remember that.

[1] ***Creatio ex nihilo***, Vol 14, No. 2, March - May 1992.

[2] Sifakis, Carl. ***American Eccentrics: Facts on File***. New York, 1984.

Chapter 3: The Fairy Tales Of Naturalism

I remember when I was a child I heard the story about the girl who found the ugly croaking frog in the pond and was disgusted by him; but then she learned that if she kissed him, he might turn into a prince. Let me tell you, that sounded like a good plan, until little girls everywhere started kissing frogs. You might also remember when a certain company produced a movie about beauty and the beast. It was the story about a hairy animal that a woman fell in love with, whereupon he became a man. I conducted an experiment. I asked several little girls at a recent revival meeting if they believed that kissing a frog would get them a boyfriend, or if a bear would turn into a man if they just fell in love with him. "No!" They said with giggles. I asked them why not; they said it was because "it's just a fairytale."

However, a frog turning into a prince is exactly what is proposed by the evolutionist. You might say, "Oh come on, Braxton, they don't teach that." Honestly, if you think about it, he adds a lot of fancy terminology and language, but that is what he is actually saying, and it shows us that evolution is indeed a fairytale. And while the evolutionist's fairy tales have gotten more elaborate, they have always been there.

In my father's book, "Spiritual Warfare," he tells of how an evolutionist professor asked him the question, "Do you know how we got a nose on our face?"

" No," my father responded.

" Well," according to my father, "This super intellectual moron said that back and back and back and back and further back than that, there was a freckle on our face and the sun began to work on that freckle and eventually a nose developed in the middle of our face." My father's reply was classic. He said, "I sure am glad that freckle wasn't on my big toe or I would have to go around smelling sweat-socks all day."

In this chapter, I want to talk to you about some fairy tales that exist even today. Additionally, I will show that if scientists would only abandon fairy tales and just follow their own scientific principles, they would find God as the cause of the universe.

Let's start at the beginning, not the beginning of life on earth, but even earlier than that. How did the universe itself come into existence? Most atheists refuse to entertain the topic and there is a reason for that. Atheism crumbles before crumbling matter even existed.

THE UNIVERSE: GETTING STARTED

What if I told you that scientifically it was more reasonable that the earthly mother of Jesus conceived him as a virgin than it is that the universe began without a cause as the evolutionist demands? I would probably be lectured on the great chasm that must exist between religion and science. However, there is something that you've got to get your mind around that is known as the "law of causality." The law of causality shows that everything that happens must have happened because something caused it to happen.

When a six- month old infant gets hit in the head with a beach ball, he turns around to look for what happened. He's actually looking for the cause of what happened. Even though he can't even talk yet, he knows that something hit him in the head and made him fall down. He also knows that the something that caused him to fall down was caused by something else. And without even thinking about it, he begins to look for what caused the ball to hit him causing him to fall down.

A child could ask the question, "Didn't the universe happen?" Of course it did. So what caused the universe? Believe it or not, many scientists who regularly depend on the law of causality say that nothing caused everything. How can they say this? Well, explanations are as wild and crazy as Aesop's fables.

Believe it or not some scientists have attempted to show what caused the universe by pointing to aliens.

LITTLE GREEN MEN

There are those scientists who explain the problem of causality by appealing to a prior intelligence that was not God but also was not human. Yes, you read that right. At the core of this argument is E.T. By the time the evolutionary scientist finishes explaining this philosophy, he will have you dazzled by his brilliance and confused by his vocabulary. Using terms like *panspermia,* the scientist will have argued that seeds were scattered throughout the universe so that there were billions of opportunities for life to begin and we just happen to be the lucky ones. Wow!

Can you just imagine what another parent would think if your child came stumbling up and asked sincerely, " Mommy, daddy, where did we come from?"

Suppose you responded by saying, " Well, Percy, billions of years ago there were these aliens who looked like giant mesquites, and they came from the planet Zenon and buried a seed in the ground, poured some miracle grow on it and we popped out." That child, the other parent and anyone else standing around would think that you were a nutcase.

But that is exactly what some evolutionists are saying. They say that some race-- not humans, not God-- came from some other planet and planted seeds here and we are the result. Richard Dawkins recently promoted this idea on an internet radio program called "the infidel guy show." I do not know of a single self respecting first grader who would believe something so silly as that; yet, it is taught in some of the most acclaimed institutes of higher learning. What is easier to believe in the beginning-- aliens or, " in the beginning God?"

After he finishes explaining all this, the super intelligent extra ignorant PhD- toting moron will sit back, remove his glasses, cross his arms and give you a condescending stare. Wait just a minute! Are you satisfied with that answer for how *everything* got started? The overconfident clergy of evolution has not explained the origin of the universe. If anything, he has only pushed it back a step. Where did the aliens come from? Who or what caused them? You might say, "Well, the same thing could be asked about God. What caused the Creator?"

On the surface, this seems like a good question. However, one thing must be understood. *The best philosophical argument for the existence of God is known as the "cosmological argument."* Time, space and matter all necessarily depend on each other. If any one of them exists, they must all exist. For this reason, the cause of any one of these elements cannot be one of them. In other words, the cause of space, time and matter must be something or someone that does not occupy space, is not confined by time and is not made of matter. Before you say, "That's something that doesn't exist," remember that the evolutionist agrees that something that doesn't exist is what the universe came from. So what is this thing? Without appealing to scripture for an answer, we can assume for now that this being or force that caused the universe is something infinite. To avoid the cosmological argument evolutionists went back to the drawing board and thought of a new possibility. What else do the scientists say might account for the universe?

The Eternal Universe

When faced with this problem, many scientists will agree that one of two things is true about the universe. Either it was caused by something infinite that exists outside of time, space and matter (which would be God), or perhaps the universe itself has always existed. Besides the fact that this isn't really an answer and it actually ignores the law of causality, there are other problems. First is the evidence that all matter is actually winding down, getting worse and will eventually decompose. If the universe had always existed, it would have done this long ago. Yet, there is a better answer that is difficult to comprehend but squashes this theory completely.

The universe cannot be infinite because if it were, we would never have arrived at today. I realize this is rather early in the book to get this abstract, but please try and follow. Imagine a line on a piece of paper that represents time. If the universe is truly infinite and has always existed, then the line would have an arrow at the left side of it to show that there never was a beginning, the line extends forever into history. Assuming that this is true, there would be an infinite number of points in history. An infinite number of points could never be traversed and thus time would never have arrived at today. It may be helpful to think of it this way:

If you were on the other side of the universe and I was here on earth, how long would it take you to get here? If we knew for sure that there were five billion miles between here and the other end of the universe, we could figure up how many thousands of years it would take; but the truth is there aren't five billion miles nor even five hundred billion miles; as far as we know there is an infinite distance and the universe extends forever. So, it would not take you a thousand years to get here or four million years. You could never get to earth because there is no other end to the universe as far as we know. So if the timeline goes into history forever and had no beginning, we could never have arrived at today. This is hard to get, but when it is comprehended, it becomes clear that the idea of an eternal universe is simply ludicrous.

One might ask the same question as before, "Don't the same rules apply to God that apply to the universe?" No, because the universe exists in time, but time as we have already shown cannot be infinite. If the being or force that caused the universe is infinite as we have said, then he or it exists outside of time. Thus, the eternal universe theory is untenable.

Simply put, they are willing to believe anything except God. That same evolutionist who explained to my father about the freckle morphing into a nose, gives us even more evidence that they would rather embrace fairytales than creation. "Have you ever wondered," he asked, "Why some people dream of falling but never hitting?"

"Well," this super sophisticated moron said, "Back and back and back and back and further back than that, our ancestors, the apes, slept in the trees, and some of the apes fell to their death and predators got them. But the other ones dreamed of falling but they never did—they are our ancestors-- and that's why you dream of falling but never hitting. Aren't you glad you know that now?"

It just goes to show they are willing to believe anything, any fairytale, but they will not accept any thing as evidence that points toward God.

Why the Confusion

The confusion surrounding this problem has daunted many creationists. Why do scientists invent these outlandish ideas of how the universe began? The answer is simple. Many scientists have an *a priori* disposition against the idea that there is a God. What is meant by this is simply that they have decided ahead of time that they will not allow the idea of God as a scientific possibility. One might say, "Well, they shouldn't because science and religion do not mix." Please remember that ideas such as this and the suggestion that religion and politics do not mix should be considered as preposterous. If God does exist, it follows simple logic that what we study about the universe he made and the government he established should have everything to do with what he has revealed to humanity about himself. Assuming that it is possible that God does exist, one could never discover the truth about the universe or its origin if God has been disqualified from the start. Still, that's exactly what scientists have done.

I want you to notice something. So far, I have not used a hint of scripture. All I have used are the laws of science with which the evolutionists themselves agree. Based on them, we have shown that the universe must have had a cause, that cause must be something that exists outside of time, space and matter which therefore means it is spiritual. That spiritual being is infinite and caused the universe to exist. All that comes from the laws of science evolutionists agree upon. Sounds a lot like the God the Bible describes, doesn't it? Well, how do we know that it is a good God or a God with a personality?

We will show in the next chapter that the chances of life arising from non-life is one chance in one to the 80th power; that is a one followed by 80 zeroes: 100,000,000,000,000,000,000,000,000,000,000,000,000,000,000,000,000,000,000,000,000,000,000,000,000,000.00 which means that it couldn't have happened on it's own. It must have had a cause that was personal.

This is what is known as the teleological argument and it goes like this: (1) something that has design must have a designer; (2) nature has design; (3) nature must have a designer.

In other words, imagine that when Bob and his wife, Julia, go home tonight and Julia finds that her makeup has spilled and her lipstick is lying next to a message on the dresser spelled out in red lipstick that says, "Julia, I can't take it anymore, go on a diet, love, Bob." I'm sure Julia is going to say, "Well, isn't it amazing my lipstick fell out and rolled around in such a way that it just randomly looks just like a message from my husband?" No! She is going to go and kill her husband because she knows he wrote a critical message about her.

She saw design in that message although it was only a sentence. In one cell of your body is the equivalent of 1,000 encyclopedias each 500 pages long; but somehow evolutionists claim it couldn't have been designed. The flagellum inside our body is more complex than a spaceship and has moving parts as well. If you look at a diagram of it, you would say it was some kind of futuristic flying car, but according to the evolutionist, it just happened by chance. If there is design, there must have been a designer.

But the evolutionist claims he sees no design. He believes things simply evolved because of slight variations over billions of years. In fact, that's why some of you are bald.

That same super sophisticated moron from before, asked this question of my father, "Do you know why it is that men go bald over time?" He continued, "It was because our ancestors, the apes, realized that if they scraped the tops of their heads against the bark of the trees and got all their hair off they were more appealing to the female apes." Of course some of you men knew that already.

It seems like some folks are willing to do whatever it takes to avoid having to believe in design because that means there is a God.

One Final Thought: The Moral Argument

C.S. Lewis was on the verge of giving up his faith in God because of all the evil in the world. Suddenly, a question occurred to him. How do I know that's evil? How do I know that some things are good and some bad? Why do I know it's wrong to steal or kill? Then it became obvious. I know because I have a moral code written in my mind. Every man has it. Even in other cultures that moral code exists. Everyone knows that certain things are right and some are wrong. Even the child knows that certain things he is doing are wrong. Someone may not know that they are sinning against a holy God, but they do seem to have a faithful internal monitor that warns them of things that shouldn't be.

A philosopher might argue that there can't be a God because if there were a God, then things wouldn't be as bad as they are in society. Wow! How does he know something is bad? He knows because he has a moral code and an understanding of justice. He has a measuring stick for good and evil, and that measuring stick is God. The moral argument demands that if man has a concept of right and wrong that is universal, it follows that a moral lawgiver placed it there. However, there were those who questioned this line of argumentation. Emil Brunner in his book, "*The Philosophy of Religion*" ponders, ". . . either the moral law is God's law. . . or the moral law is really a law given by ourselves, and the intelligible ego is our own deepest ego, in which case we have no serious knowledge of either evil or God".[1] But this fails to address the claim that no law exists without a lawgiver. Lewis explains, "My argument against God was that the universe seemed so cruel and unjust. But how had I got this idea of just and unjust? A man does not call a line crooked unless he has some idea of a straight line. . . Consequently atheism turns out to be too simple."[2] Understanding Lewis' argument, it becomes clear that general revelation leads any reasoning man to find a God who exists outside of time, space and matter, is creative in nature and is personal because he has written a moral code onto the minds of all men. I hope that you will recognize that all evolutionists have to offer are fairytales. God is offering us a story that will never change.

[1]Brunner, Emil. ***The Philosophy of Religion***. James Clarke & co. ltd.

[2]Lewis, C.S. ***Mere Christianity.*** Harper.

Chapter 4: The Answer to Naturalism

When I was a teenager and just beginning to date girls, my father gave me many little nuggets of wisdom to remember. One thing he told me was that I should never talk about a girl's size or weight. You and I know that this is good advice, but I thought, "My father doesn't know everything. Girls today are different than they used to be." I ignored all of his wisdom until one day I made a terrible mistake. While riding in the car with a girl, I realized she was having trouble buckling her seat belt. Finally I reached over, grabbed hold of it, readjusted the length and clipped it in saying, "I'm sorry. I guess the last girl that rode here was not quite as big as you." Huge mistake! It would have been better if I had believed my father's words from the start without any proof, but when I saw the evidence, I would never again forget.

A similar thing is happening in Christianity today. We communicate with others who believe like us so often that we forget that some people do not accept the Bible as wholeheartedly as we do. Our Bible says, " In the beginning God created the heavens and the earth." It would be best if they believed without the evidence, at least that's what Jesus told Thomas. But some scientists today, like Dr. Richard Dawkins, demand that the universe is all that really exists. The question is, "How will we as Christian respond?"

"For the invisible things of him from the creation of the world are clearly seen, being understood by the things that are made, even his eternal power and Godhead; so that they are without excuse:" (Romans 1:20)

Scripture is clear that there is no excuse for the atheist. It is clear that there is a God. In fact, the Bible goes so far as to say that it is obvious that there is a God. That is enough for a lot of Christians. Many of my contemporaries, and even some of the ministers whom I admire the most, have in the past demanded that we must simply accept all of this on faith without a shred of evidence. But that is not what the Bible says.

"But sanctify the Lord God in your hearts: and be ready always to give an answer to every man that asketh you a reason of the hope that is in you with meekness and fear:" (1 Peter 3:15)

If you look at these two verses, it becomes clear that Christians are required to show those who are not believers why it is obvious that there is a God. Just like my date in the car, once they see the evidence that what we have been saying is true, there is a much better chance they will remember it. Showing them the evidence is not as impossible as you might think.

I'm sure that you know how your home came into existence. Well, if we are to take the reasoning of the atheist, there was an explosion in a brick factory and your house, apartment complex or condominium was the natural result. Of course, you would never believe that. You know that intelligent design went into building that structure. Or consider Mount Rushmore. How did the presidents' images get there? Don't you think it is quite possible that millions of years of erosion, wind and water working on the side of that rocky face resulted in the image of the presidents? Such a proposal would be ridiculous. It is clear that there was a designer. Scientists are thrilled when they discover an Indian arrow head, and yet the only reason they are able to determine it was designed by intelligence is that it has a few spots that have been chipped away.

In years past, it seemed obvious to people of faith that there was a designer simply because just as cars have design and trains have design our bodies seem to have design as well. This is the teleological argument mentioned in the last chapter. But now there are answers to this argument coming from atheists.

In his book, *The Blind Watchmaker,* Richard Dawkins, a hero of evolution, says this, "We have seen that living things are too improbable and too beautifully 'designed' to have come into existence by chance. How, then, did they come into existence? The answer, Darwin's answer, is by gradual, step-by-step transformations from simple beginnings, from primordial entities sufficiently simple to have come into existence by chance."[1]

How do you deal with that argument?

Ken Ham is a creation theologian with whom I am in disagreement on several points. Nevertheless he and the microbiologist Michael Behe have written extensively on this subject and so a look at some of their explanations is prudent here. Ken Ham has said, "Life is built upon the basis of that molecule heredity, DNA. All your genes and all your cells come from that double helix of information. In fact, it has been estimated that if you just took one of your trillions of cells and typed out the information it takes to make you. it would fill a thousand books that are five hundred pages each and closed type written. There is a lot of information inside of you. It got there by chance, huh? And this is how it's explained. With Morse code, you could take beads on a rope and write words, couldn't you? In a crude sense, a molecule has information lined up on it, millions of lines of information that make up what you are. Now a teacher will say, 'Look, you don't have to believe in God. As long as by chance those molecules line up in the right order, you can get life. Lets look at it kids,' the teacher says, 'Put all the letters of the alphabet in a hat and pass the hat around the class and three students in a row pull out the letters at random B-A-T. What's that spell, kids—'bat.' So, you can get words by chance, and you could possibly get sentences by chance, and even though it seems improbable, it's still remotely possible you could get the encyclopedia. As long as you get the right line up of information, you can get life. Students, you don't need God."

That's how kids are taught, and as ridiculous as it seems already, there is something terribly wrong with that analogy. Who recognizes that word, "bat"? A Frenchman, Chinese, Mexican? Only an English speaking person recognizes that word, someone who has already got the language. This is what Michael Behe calls, "*irreducible complexity.*"

We know that in a human cell there is a language system. There are also other chemicals that read the DNA that makes the language system. So, there is a language and there is something that reads it, and both are necessary. In other words, it all must be there from the start. One part doesn't work without all the parts.

Some creationists have explained the idea of irreducible complexity by asking the question, "Are you aware that a 747 is an airplane that flies, but it's made up of six million parts? Furthermore, did you know that not one of those six million parts flies?" Now that's something to think about the next time you fly in a 747 at 35,000 feet. You are flying in something of which not one part flies. Life is no different. Everything must be in place from the start or else it will not survive.

Perhaps the most annoying creature on the planet is the fly. Imagine that as a biology teacher explained the intricacies of the evolutionary process to her class, one of the students noticed a fly creeping about on his biology textbook. Squashing the fly with great enthusiasm, the student would have created an incredible biological specimen. If he had the wherewithal to challenge the liberal doctrine of his educational establishment, he could have asked a couple of poignant questions of his teacher. First, he could ask, "Teacher, if the textbook is true, will this fly ever fly again?" Without even requiring a response, it is clear the answer is, "no." The class would indeed cackle at the idea. However, if the textbook is right, then one could never hope to find a more appropriate primordial soup than what is present in front of the student. All the proper nutrients are there and even the DNA is there, but the problem is that the student *rearranged* the information. In fact, it wouldn't fly if left alone for ten minutes or ten billion years.

Life is no different than a machine; it must be ordered by an intelligent being. We all agree that a 747 has to have all its parts present before a flight is attempted or else it doesn't fly. In the same way, just one cell in the human body is as complex as thousands of 747s all communicating with each other using a specific language that they all understand, and it all necessarily had to be there in the beginning. With blind random chance it doesn't work.

Perhaps the greatest example of something that could not have evolved is the bacterial motor called the flagellum. Like the 747, the flagellum functions like a machine, meaning that each part had to be in place from the start or it would never have worked. This tiny mechanism consists of about forty complex protein parts all of which interact with each other and are necessary. The absence of any one of these parts would result in a nonworking flagellum. If a flagellum were drawn on a chalk board, or a diagram were shown, you would think it was some kind of futuristic spaceship. Looking like something from NASA, it is aerodynamic, complicated, mechanical and even has functioning parts for propulsion. Similarly, the animal cell's cilium is like an oar that whips back and forth and consists of 200 working parts, all of which are necessary for functionality. The point is that one small part of this device couldn't have slowly evolved because each part had to be there from the start in order to work at all.

Then, of course, there is the human eye. Evolutionists have long sought to explain how this extremely complex device works. How could the human eye have formed through random variations over billions of years? Richard Dawkins gave an answer that has been accepted by several scientists and claims that a grouping of light-sensitive cells grew stronger, and as they did natural selection created all of the component parts. Without explaining where these light-sensitive cells came from, or how natural selection developed the component parts, Dawkins claims that all of this was proven through a computer simulation. However, no one has been able to discover this elusive computer simulation, and when David Berlinski took up the task of researching it, he decided that the whole thing was an urban myth.

Whether it is the flagellum, the cilium, the eye or something else, certain biological devices are so complex that like an airplane they must have all the fully finished parts in working order before they begin. Evolution can't explain these irreducibly complex things.

Already the walls of the evolutionary religion are crumbling and it is important for you to notice that I have not made an appeal to scripture even once for evidence. So far all we have said is that life relies on organisms that function as machines, meaning that each part had to be in working order from the start in order for life to begin. This is something that Charles Darwin himself explained would debunk his entire theory if ever proven when he said:

"If it could be demonstrated that any complex organ existed which could not possibly have been formed by numerous, successive, slight modifications, my theory would absolutely break down."[2]

The evolutionist teaches that information just keeps getting more complex and more complex throughout history and things are getting better and better which is totally contrary to reality. Instead, things are getting worse and winding down. It is explained by saying mutations cause these occurrences. You've heard of mutations, haven't you? If you've heard of Michael Jackson, you've heard of mutations. They say that these mutations will produce new information, but that has never happened. It just rearranged information that was already there. No new information was created.

Dogs turn into dogs, cats turn into cats, but dogs do not turn into cats or pigs or bananas.

    The thing that I want you to understand more than anything else is that the danger of evolution is so prominent because throughout modern history Christians have looked to science and tried to make the Bible fit with it rather than letting the Bible speak for itself. Friends, the truth is that the Bible has not changed in thousands of years while the textbook changes every couple of semesters. As I said in the introduction, general revelation (what we see in nature) and special revelation (what God has specifically said to us) should be balanced together. I contend that if a man measures what we know for sure about nature against what we know for sure about the teaching of the Bible they will always be in harmony.

    The real problem is that many Christians have done what Scofield and others did. They asserted that God created the heaven and the earth, but when asked about the events of Genesis chapters 1-11 and whether or not they are to be taken literally, many of these same Christians will say, "Ah, I don't know that there was really an Adam and Eve. I don't know that there was really a Noah's ark." And whether they realize it or not, they are saying this because the church has started teaching that certain things in Genesis aren't to be taken literally so that there is room for evolution.

At this point, special revelation can be allowed to enter the debate for two reasons. (1) It has been demonstrated in the previous chapters that there must be a theistic designer by virtue of the laws of science (specifically the law of causality) and Michael Behe's theory of irreducible complexity. (2) Because it has been argued that biblical creation more adequately fits with what we know of science, we may logically step forth *to see if* special revelation continues to complement the scientific world.

Jesus quoted Genesis as history; so did Paul. When my wife and I were in Rome, we read a plaque that said, "Caesar took this many men and this many horses and went in this direction." What if I had said to the person next to me, "I wonder what it means 'horses,' I wonder what it means ' men,' and I wonder what it means 'Caesar?" The man next to me would have said, "Are you nuts?" I would respond by telling him that I was just trying to understand what the author is saying. What do you think it means? It means what it says. It means Caesar took some horses and went over there. The same thing is true of the ark. God placed a door on the ark. What do you think that means? I think it means there was a door on the ark. It says in Noah's day there was a great flood; what do you think that means? I think it means there was a flood and it happened while a guy named Noah was alive. Genesis is a history book and should be read as history.

One of the great problems with churches all over America regarding the doctrines of extreme Calvinism, works-based salvation and baptismal regeneration is that we don't want to read God's Word and let him speak to us. We want to read God's word and tell him what he means.

I will guarantee you that every church in this nation that condones homosexuality is a church that doesn't believe that the first eleven chapters of Genesis are to be taken literally. Every major doctrine of the Bible is first found in Genesis, and if you remove it, you have cut the heart out of the Bible. That is why the humanists are so serious about protecting evolution and keeping these things fairy tales. After all, if you can't trace all of humanity back to one man, then who are we. We get so much from Genesis. Ken Ham argues this point well during his speaking engagements. Why did God kill an animal and use its skin to clothe Adam and Eve? The answer is given in Hebrews 9 which says, "Without the shedding of blood there is no remission." For the same reason, Jesus had to come as the second Adam to die and cover the sins of the world. Why could our sins have not been covered by an animal sacrifice? Because we are not animals; we were made in the image of God and thus needed a God-sacrifice to cover our sins and to clothe our spiritual nakedness.

You might say, "That doesn't make any sense." Sure it does. Norman Geisler says that to put a puzzle together properly, you need the right boxtop to follow. Evolutionists and creationists have the same pieces of the puzzle; we are just looking at different boxtops. If you are looking at a boxtop that is wrong, you're never going to get anywhere. Evolutionists refuse to look at the right boxtop, God's boxtop, and if they ever did, the pieces would all begin to fit.

You might say, "I don't like God's boxtop; it has pain and hunger and misery." You must understand that human suffering is the result of sin, and if you believe in Christianity and try to believe that man evolved, then you believe that death and disease were all around before the fall of man; yet, God said everything was good. If you believe the evolutionist, you call God a liar because everything was not good. Sin wrecked the world.

I heard about a boy who saw all the beautiful statues in Rome. He continued into the Vatican and saw all the gorgeous statues with missing arms and chipped away spots. Someone commented on the beauty and he said, "I don't know; it all looks broken to me."

It is all broken, and the world we live in was once beautiful and we see inklings of that beauty, but it is not the beautiful world it once was There are diseases, earthquakes, pain, death and misery because it is a distorted, sin-wrecked version of what God created. It was a beautiful world originally but now it is warped.

When a prominent young person in our city ended his own life, some of the educators who observed him said that his death was the result of natural evolution. Weak people who cannot handle stress will not survive. You know the truth is that evolution is the cause of amoral young people today, not because evolution is real, but rather because it has been hammered into the students' heads with the inevitable result that they view life as having no moral absolutes. They are being taught to make up their own standard of ethics.

People all over television say they want morality back in school. I would ask what morality, whose morality? Who gets to decide what is right and what is wrong. What they really want are the beautiful essences of Christianity but you can't have Christianity without Christ and the Bible and the Ten Commandments. So people throw it all out.

And the more that you tell a kid that there are no absolutes and that man is just an animal, the kid will begin to think nobody owns me so I'll do what I want.

Abortion is not the problem in America today; homosexuality is not the problem; drugs are not the problem-- they are all symptoms. The problem is that people no longer accept the authority of the Word of God. How do we fix the problems in the world today? Here is how. Preach the Word of God, because if you tell people they are wrong, they'll say, "Why?" The obvious answer to some is to say, "The Bible says so."

To that they will probably reply, "Well, that's just a religious book; it was proven wrong long ago by science. Where's the evidence of a global flood? Where did all the water go? What about dinosaurs? They're proof of billions of years of evolution. What about the fossil record?"

What are you going to tell them? We had better understand the Bible. Science books are revised every couple of years. Scripture is always the same.

Understanding all of this, it is needful to make comment about a philosophy known as theistic evolution. There are those who profess to be believers who believe in the absolute authority of the Bible while also holding to the principles of evolution. How this cocktail of beliefs is arrived at or is reconciled with scripture is not the subject of our debate. Yet, many Christians write these individuals off as unsaved. I can only offer my opinion. I believe that this view is wrong, but wrongness does not necessarily equal lostness. We should be increasingly cautious about saying someone is not truly a Christian simply because they have a slightly differing view of things than do we.

In these first four chapters we have seen the blinding lights of creation. Glaring evidences that God exists have been demonstrated and shown plausible. Moreover, it would seem that the idea of a designer for the universe exists beyond a reasonable doubt. However, before moving on to the next section, one final argument must be considered. There is a philosophical idea that would (if true) cause logic a great deal of difficulty, and that idea is called relativism. Thus, before moving on to the evidences for the divinity of Jesus Christ, this philosophy must be debunked. Hence, the next chapter will be devoted to the three forms of relativism.

1 Dawkins, Richard. ***The Blind Watchmaker***. USA Publisher: W.W. Norton & Company

[2] Darwin, Charles. ***The Origin of Species***. Reprint of 1st ed. (Cambridge, MA:

Harvard university Press, 1964).

Chapter 5: Relativism

What does the word "truth" really mean? Philosophers have often considered this and attempted to classify those things which may be regarded as true. Leave it to philosophers to make the obvious seem abstract. The things that may be classified as true are things that happen to be true. Many people have arms and legs, trees have branches, humans need oxygen, wood burns, birds fly and liberal men are pansies. You see, there are many things that are objectively true. However, there is great contention among modern day thinkers about whether truth actually exists. Is anything really true? "There is no absolute truth," is the definitive statement from those today holding the position known as relativism. In this chapter, I will explain how this philosophy and the variations of it are truly and absolutely ridiculous.

There are three major classifications of relativism that are recognizable in the world today. These divisions are cognitive relativism, moral relativism and situational relativism. Let's jump in with that order in mind.

Cognitive Relativism

Cognitive relativism is the dumbest of the three. I'm sorry. I attempted to write this section three times without being offensive and blunt as, Ravi Zacharias, C.S. Lewis and others have. I'm just simply not one of those great gentlemen. Either cognitive relativists are lacking the mental faculties to think logically or they have purposefully and deceitfully claimed this position for God knows why.

Simply put, this argument claims that nothing is absolutely true. The ideas that the world is round, people die, babies are born, 1 + 1 = 2 and that people even exist are all relative. Often the phrase will be heard, "That may be true for you, but it's not true for me." How silly! 1 +1 = 2 is true even if you're an alien from another planet where everyone is a relativist. It is always true, it has always been true, it will always be true and there is no way to make it untrue. In fact, the very statement that there is no absolute truth is an absolute statement.

I feel that I am insulting the reader by even discussing this harebrained philosophy, but unfortunately it demands attention. Why? On college campuses across America today, it is all the rage to be a cognitive relativist. If you don't like Christianity, you can simply opt out of the argument by claiming, "Well that is true for you but not me." If you don't like Islam but don't know how to address it, then just back away with the same senseless statement as before. If a logically thinking person (how dare they seek higher education) confronts you that your personal belief makes no sense and is bad for you and everyone else, why not sound open-minded by complimenting them on their truth and then explaining that its just not true for everyone? There is no end to this insanity. It is the murder of logic.

Imagine that a teacher grades the paper of a relativist who writes on that very subject and assigns the student an "F." The student would surely complain that this just isn't right. The paper was well put together and carefully thought out. So the teacher responds, "You submitted it in a blue folder and I personally prefer red." The student would demand that's just wrong. Wouldn't it be great to hear the teacher say, "Well, I guess your truth is just different than mine." Do you think that's ridiculous? It's the actual event described by Norman Geisler in his book "*I Don't Have Enough Faith to be an Atheist.*" So why do we know that truth is not relative.

As already demonstrated, mathematics is the best purveyor of absolute truth. It is the universal language and is always constant. It is completely objective, cannot be argued with and will always result in the predicted answer if performed properly. If one single number was relative and not constant our universe would cease in some unimaginable way. Everything, not most things, depends on absolute truth.

I began my ministry working with youth and people often ask me, "Why did you go on to being a pastor rather than continuing in the youth ministry?" They usually assume that God called me to be a pastor. Honestly, I hope that that is the case and I know that he eventually did call me to the work of a pastor. Nevertheless, when I left youth ministry originally, it was because I could no longer stand the underdeveloped arguments of so many of the teenagers I knew. Thank God that he is moving in a new way among young people now. There is a craving for knowledge that exists. However, as I write this, those of you for whom I was responsible are in universities seeking masters degrees and associating with so many foolish relativists, I urge young people reading this book to think logically, basing everything you believe on facts and evidences including what you believe about God.

MORAL RELATIVISM

Only slightly more logical is the idea that though there is objective truth for many things, there is not for morals or ethics. That is to say, what is wrong, sinful or wicked for me to do may not be for someone else. Sadly, even Christians often align themselves with this senseless philosophy. Some will say, "Sexual activity prior to marriage is wrong for those who are convicted that it is, but for me it must not be wrong because it feels so right." Similar arguments are made for smoking, drinking, lying, cheating financially, gambling, not attending church, enjoying sinful entertainment and a host of other issues. So what's wrong with this argument?

Acceptable as it may seem, the problem is that nothing else about the world seems to fit with such a philosophy. By this I mean that we see absolute truth represented in the ordinary events of life: gravity, math, causality and others. Absolutism is also seen in social constraints. For example, it is absolutely true that if you murder, you have broken the law. You may not receive proper punishment, but the law exists absolutely. So, if there are absolute truths about science and philosophy, why do we demand that this is not true of morals?

Most of the time this argument is made because of the seeming differences among cultures regarding ethics. We would say that labeling cannibalism as immoral is true for Americans while some tribes deep in South American jungles see this as a holy rite. Arguing for this position, some would say that the South Americans are not immoral for doing what is true for them. Moreover, the use of marijuana for recreation is arguably accepted as immoral in America while some areas of Canada and Amsterdam view it as a common social lubricant. Conversely, in America, women can move about in public without enough fabric covering them to make a hummingbird a decent outfit, while in Iran a woman would face serious punishment for doing the same. Homosexuality is becoming more accepted every day among Americans (at least in blue states) while in 2005, the Bahamian government refused to allow a cruise ship filled with gay and lesbian passengers headed by Rosie O'Donnell (the lesbian mother Teresa) to even dock in their port.

Clearly, there is a difference in the stated values of various countries. Isn't this a plausible argument for moral relativism? No! Remember, these are the different "stated" values and performed actions of different people groups, but that does not mean that they are morally relative. Consider the South Americans' involvement in cannibalism. While this is an accepted practice among them, they follow it with a ritual of purification because of the evil of devouring a human. Bazaar religious views have kept cannibalism alive, but the moral dilemmas faced by social groups worldwide regarding the sanctity of human life has driven them to seek forgiveness from their gods by way of ritual sanctification.

Marijuana is thought to be neither moral nor immoral by many because of their own desires to get wasted or their libertarian views, but potheads from any country share one thing in common with our South American friends. They are ashamed of their habit. If you ask the average user in Amsterdam whether he uses marijuana, he may admit that he does, but only after turning red and looking embarrassed. Granted, there are exceptions, but we may establish a moral principle by viewing its presence in the majority. The same shameful attitude can be witnessed among women who dress like prostitutes.

The exception would seem to be homosexuality. Gay pride is on the rampage. I want to make a statement now that may seem to promote this lifestyle although that is not the intent. I am broken hearted by the treatment homosexuals receive from church-goers. At what point did it become right for believers to treat gays and lesbians with less love than we do adulterers, drug addicts, gossipers, cheaters, liars, thieves and others? If you are a homosexual reader, please do not feel that I am equating you with these sorts of sinners. The problem is that although the God of the Bible speaks clearly in both testaments that this is an immoral practice, the approach Christians take should not be harsher than with regard to any other immoral behavior. Homosexuals should be loved back to Christ. I realize I am on a rabbit trail, but remember, I am a vocational Christian speaker and that is my prerogative.

I am personally ashamed of the immoral way believers have responded to the homosexual movement. While I align my political and spiritual views with the church, I cannot condone their ridiculous personal views. Too many believers are afraid to witness or even speak to homosexuals for the most outlandish reasons. I assure you, the vast majority of homosexual men and women are not child molesters and you will not become gay by speaking to them. A gay man will not want to be romantic with you, sir, simply because you are a man anymore than most women want to be romantic with you. Am I defending the lifestyle? Not as a morally acceptable one. I am however, defending these human beings from Christian religious hatred when they should be influenced with love.

Still, the fact remains that homosexuality seems morally relative because even the homosexual seems proud of his life choice. It should be understood that this was not always the case. Only since the outspoken left has declared the validity of this way of life, began throwing gay pride parades, promoted entertainment that is gay-friendly, and viciously attacked anyone who seemed too straight has it become wrong not to be proud of being a homosexual. Government schools have not helped the matter either. Still, homosexuals, by and large, are ashamed. Don't take my word for it, take the word of wayne Besen author of "Anything But Straight: Unmasking the Scandals and Lies Behind the Ex-Gay Myth"[1] who spoke out against ministries that seek to help homosexuals. He said they usually end up ". . . exacerbating the aloneness a homosexual **ashamed** of his or her orientation might feel" (emphasis mine). Clearly, in clinical discussions about the matter, even gay advocates accept that homosexuals are ashamed of the lifestyle. This becomes even more visible when honest former gays speak out about their past. In his article, "Confession From A Former Homosexual," Richard Weller explains, "I love and respect myself today, but I hate the things that I used to do. Homosexual sexuality is perverse and unhealthy, both physically and emotionally. We put on such a respectable image, but inside we were miserable and ashamed." [2]

The trend I want you to notice is that within every culture and people group in the world, the same moral outline may be uncovered despite the laws and actions taken. The way they may be uncovered is not to notice the lifestyle but rather the attitude the individual has about his lifestyle.

What is the result of this test? The morals and ethics discovered in the Bible are the very ones written on every human heart. This was the basis of C.S. Lewis' most notable apologetic work, "Mere Christianity." Moral truth is not relative because people are ashamed of their sin.

SITUATIONAL RELATIVISM

A final question for consideration is this: "Is truth relative to a given situation?" You might be more of a proponent of this than you think. Usually, it is morally wrong to lie. However, the situation might occur wherein lying would be the most loving thing to do. The common example is that of a woman asking her husband if she looks fat, and she does. In this case the idea that you should always tell the truth seems flawed. Thus truth is relative to a situation. The problem is that this argument is based on a faulty assumption. The assumption is that the woman would benefit from being lied to. In reality (though this won't win me any points with the female crowd) it might be a great opportunity to sit down and talk about a family fitness plan.

Our judicial system in America is meant to support the idea of constant truth within all situations. In the event that some third party might be in jeopardy if a particular witness chooses to tell the truth, it might seem best to lie. Indeed, even the witnesses themselves may be in jeopardy, and thus the Fifth Amendment is present, so that rather than lying the witness may simply not answer. If your mother ever said, "If you can't say something nice don't say anything at all," she was right. Based on what we have already demonstrated about truth, it is clear that it is not relative. If truth is always the moral centerpiece, then just as with moral relativism, it is not logical to say that in some cases it is not virtuous. It either is or it is not. However, truth is not the only thing that is considered situational by the relativist.

Abortion is the flagship for situational relativists today. Many Christians will suggest that although abortion is morally reprehensible, it is sometimes necessary. What if a girl is raped and as a result becomes pregnant? Shouldn't she be allowed to have an abortion so that she may have a fair chance at life? No! Two wrongs do not make a right. And moreover, while the girl may have a fair chance at life, the child never had the chance to be born. Its rights have been violated before it could even speak for them. Situational relativism just doesn't hold up.

More should be said about the issue of abortion. I understand that even some believers in Christianity hold that abortion isn't sinful at all. The fetus (at least in its early stages) is nothing more than a collection of cells with neither cognitive thought nor self awareness. Based on this, it could be said that abortion is not murder. However, there is a great assumption made here that can not be proved. It has been assumed that the collection of cells does not constitute human life in science or the eyes of God. How do we know that? Where is the logic of that argument? Some would respond that pro-life advocates cannot logically say that God does consider the fetus to be a human life. Perhaps this is true. What is factual and certain is that no one (without special revelation) knows if it is a life or not. So what?

Imagine that standing before you was a booth with no windows. You have no idea and no way of knowing if someone is standing inside that booth or not. However, the booth is in your way and it would be much more convenient if the booth was removed. Now you have a choice. With the push of a button you may destroy the booth and its potential contents. Should you destroy the booth that may have someone inside? Absolutely not. If you did this and there was someone inside, you would be a murderer. What about someone's right to choose what is convenient? In this case, that philosophy would fly right out the window.

The same predicament exists with abortion. The woman considering an abortion is considering the demolition of a booth that may contain a human life. Maybe it does and maybe it doesn't. Remember, there is no scientific way of knowing if the fetus is a human being or not. Therefore, the woman has two competing virtues with which she is faced. On the one hand, the virtue of liberty exists. People should be free to make choices. Conversely, there is the virtue of human life. Logically, in this case, the woman ought to choose the virtue of human life over the virtue of human liberty. Even so, liberal thinking has promoted the idea that the virtue of human liberty should win out over the virtue of human life, demanding that the woman have the right to blow up the booth and potentially commit murder. Honestly, I challenge anyone to refute this logic. It is asinine to think any differently. This is not a matter of opinion; it is a matter of fact.

I have often heard people say, "I think abortion is wrong, but I don't think I should keep someone else from choosing." Tell me, would it be wrong for you to stop someone from exploding the booth that might contain a man? Indeed, we should restrain someone physically from doing such a thing. If they chose to do this, whether or not there was a man in the booth, we could at the most charge them with attempted murder and at the least with reckless endangerment even if it was devoid of a person. I'm not advocating the violence of extremist Christian groups who bomb abortion clinics, but I am making a plea for logic and sobriety in this matter. What does this have to say for situational relativism? Understanding that this is true, murder is never okay. It is not okay to murder out of convenience and it is not okay to murder if a young girl is raped. You might say, "What if it isn't murder?" My response would be, "Prove to me evidentially that it is not." You can't.

Each of these three philosophies of relativism exists for the same reason-- to justify sin. If we can establish that truth is a matter of opinion, culture or situation, then we may do whatever we choose to do without regard for what God may think. It, like all sin, is the spawn of selfishness. Truth is the greatest blinding light that you will ever encounter. It cannot be squelched nor dimmed. It exposes all and in this case is the glaring evidence that relativism is illogical.

[1] Besen, Wayne. ***Anything But Straight: Unmasking the Scandals and Lies Behind the Ex-***

Gay Myth. Harrington Park Press.

[2] Weller, Richard. ***Confession from a Former Homosexual***. March 28, 2002

NewsWithViews.com

SECTION 2

The laws of science are true. Science and religion are not competitors but companions. In Section One, we detailed the means by which man can know beyond a reasonable doubt that God exists according to the laws of science. He must exist. If the laws that are discoverable about our universe are true, he cannot not exist. Understanding that relativism is senseless, we may also conclude that a universe with a personal and real God is the only one that can exist.

However, this is only the first step. Knowing that there is a God is vastly different than knowing God. Indeed, there are innumerable ideas about what God or gods there are. For this reason, in Section Two, we will remain in the discussion of general revelation and seek to establish through natural evidences that Jesus is the one true God. As we continue, remember; this is not special revelation. We are arguing for the veracity of Jesus without appealing to the idea that the Bible must be God's Word. However, by the end of Section Two, it is my belief that the lights of biblical evidence will be so blinding that you will be convinced of the truth of God's Word and thus we will bridge the gap between general revelation (what is known about God from observing the universe) and special revelation (what is known about God through divine speech/scripture).

Chapter 6: The Prophecies Surrounding His Life

So now what? It has been demonstrated that the universe likely came into being as the result of a creator, but that's just the beginning. There are countless religions that believe in some sort of god. Shutting the door on natural evolution doesn't answer the question of who God is or how man can know him. Indeed, there are even countless versions of what kind of god or gods may exist. Most people have at least heard of Jesus, Alla and Zeus. Surprisingly, many people feel like just a few gods like these are the only ones vying for existence in the world of religion. Shocking to most is the truth that there are as many gods and views of gods as there are churches in the south. Henotheism, polytheism, monotheism, deism, atheism, hemitheism, pantheism and a host of other views describe the ideas that exist about the divine. Who has got the real God(s)? Who knows?

Actually, there is one way of discovering the answer. What if writers were able to predict that God would come and live on earth? In fact, while we're fantasizing, what if they were able to predict where he would be born who would associate with him, what he would preach how he would die, what the specific condition of his body would be when he died, what the exact date of his death would be as well as about 295 other facts about him at least 400 years before he was born. Wouldn't that be great! If that were true, we might as well forget everything else--that man would undoubtedly be God. Believe it or not, those facts are exactly what the Old Testament contains.

You might say, "Sure, but how do I know that authors didn't come along years after Jesus and just make all the prophecies fit his life exactly?" You would have had a point prior to 1947. That was the year that a young man wondering around the cliff walls that surround the Dead Sea made a world changing discovery. He told reporters later that he had tossed a stone into the cave and heard something shatter. Upon closer investigation, he found clay jars filled with manuscripts of the Old Testament. Holding the strips of material in his hands, the young man had no idea that he was holding the evidence that would convince thousands of people to trust Christ as their savior. How did it get there? A strange group of people who write everything down had once called this place home. No, not lawyers, but Essenes.

The area called Qumram had been home to a community of people called the Essenes. Considered strange by the others of their time, they had unusual views of what it meant to be a Jew serving Jehovah. It has been speculated that this group of people living in the wilderness accepted John the Baptist among their ranks until the time that he would "make a way" for Christ. However, the important issue is that these people were writers. Anything they could document, they did. When Qumram was excavated, scrolls were found every few feet buried in the dirt or in caves. When an Israeli is asked about the Essenes living in Qumram, he will tell you, "Oh yes, those people who walked around with scrolls falling off of them everywhere."

Praise God for the Essenes. Because they collected and created documents with such fervor, we now have what are called the Dead Sea Scrolls. So what? What are they? Many have criticized the Old Testament prophecies saying, "These are too exact, someone must have doctored these writings after the time of Christ to include such specific information about him." Such an idea was accepted among philosophers prior to the discovery of the scrolls. The Dead Sea Scrolls contain prophecies that date to a time prior to the life of Christ. Resulting from this is absolute evidence that the prophecies came true.

Unbelievable as it may sound, the greatest prophecies of all time have been undeniably proven. Most non-Christian philosophers today admittedly have no answer to this dilemma. Those who try to criticize the dating of the Dead Sea Scrolls are quickly discredited by their peers. Others have attempted to dodge the bullet by claiming that the prophecies are too vague and could have referred to anyone. You be the judge. Below is a list of the shocking prophecies that have already been verified as factual and in most cases exact.

Old Testament Scriptures That Describe The Coming Messiah		
The Messianic Prophecy	Where the prophecy appears in the Old Testament (written between 1450 BC and 430BC)	Jesus' fulfillment of the prophecy in the New Testament (written between 45 and 95 AD)
He will be in the family of Eve	Genesis 3:15	Galatians 4:4

He will be a descendant of Abraham and a relief to the world	Genesis 12:3; 18:18	Acts 3:25,26
He will be of the tribe of Judah	Genesis 49:10	Matthew 1:2 and Luke 3:33
He will be a prophet like Moses	Deuteronomy 18:15-19	Acts 3:22,23
He will be the Son of God	Psalm 2:7	Matthew 3:17; Mark 1:11; Luke 3:22
He will be resurrected	Psalm 16:10,11 and 49:15	Matthew 28:5-9; Mark 16:6; Luke 24:4-7; John 20:11-16; Acts 1:3 and 2:32
He will be specifically crucified	Psalm 22 (contains 11 prophecies—not all listed here)	Matthew 27:34-50 and John 19:17-30
He will be humiliated and mocked	Psalm 22:7	Luke 23:11,35-39
He will be pierced through hands and feet	Psalm 22:16	Luke 23:33 and 24:36-39; John 19:18 and 20:19-20,24-27
Though he will be crucified and beaten, his bones will not be broken	Psalm 22:17 and 34:20	John 19:31-33,36

Men will gamble for His clothing	Psalm 22:18	Matthew 27:35; Mark 15:24; Luke 23:34; John 19:23,24
He will be accused by liars	Psalm 35:11	Matthew 26:59,60 and Mark 14:56,57
The Messiah will be hated without a cause	Psalm 35:19 and 69:4	John 15:23-25
He will be betrayed by a friend	Psalm 41:9	John 13:18,21
He will ascend to heaven	Psalm 68:18	Luke 24:51; Acts 1:9; 2:33-35; 3:20-21; 5:31,32; 7:55-56; Romans 8:34; Ephesians 1:20,21; Colossians 3:1; Hebrews 1:3; 8:1; 10:12; 12:2; 1 Pet 3:22
He will be given vinegar and gall to drink	Psalm 69:21	Matthew 27:34; Mark 15:23; John 19:29,30
Kings will respect and worship Him	Psalm 72:10,11	Matthew 2:1-11
He is a "stone the builders rejected" who will become the "chief cornerstone"	Psalm 118:22,23 and Isaiah 28:16	Matthew 21:42,43; Acts 4:11; Ephesians 2:20; 1 Peter 2:6-8

He will be a descendant of David	Psalm 132:11 and Jeremiah 23:5,6; 33:15,16	Luke 1:32,33
He will be born of a virgin	Isaiah 7:14	Matthew 1:18-25 and Luke 1:26-35
His first miracle will be in Galilee	Isaiah 9:1-7	Matthew 4:12-16
He will heal the blind and the deaf	Isaiah 35:5-6	Many places. Also see Matthew 11:3-6 and John 11:47
He will be scourged, humiliated, and spat upon	Isaiah 50:6	Matthew 26:67 and 27:26-31
The "Gospel according to Isaiah"	Isaiah 52:13-53:12	Matthew, Mark, Luke, John
People will hear and not believe the "arm of the LORD" (Messiah)	Isaiah 53:1	John 12:37,38
He will be rejected	Isaiah 53:3	Matthew 27:20-25; Mark 15:8-14; Luke 23:18-23; John 19:14,15
He will be killed	Isaiah 53:5-9	Matthew 27:50; Mark 15:37-39; Luke 23:46; John 19:30
He will silently listen as he is accused	Isaiah 53:7	Matthew 26:62,63 and 27:12-14

He will be buried with the rich	Isaiah 53:9	Matthew 27:59,60; Mark 15:46; Luke 23:52,53; John 19:38-42
He will be crucified with criminals	Isaiah 53:12	Matthew 27:38; Mark 15:27; Luke 23:32,33
He is part of the new covenant	Isaiah 55:3-4 and Jeremiah 31:31-34	Matthew 26:28; Mark 14:24; Luke 22:20; Hebrews 8:6-13
He will be our Advocate	Isaiah 59:16	Hebrews 9:15
He has a dual purpose	Isaiah 61:1-3 (His first purpose will end at the ". . . year of the Lord's favor")	Luke 4:16-21; His second purpose will be completed at the end of time
He will arrive at a specified time	Daniel 9:25-26	Galatians 4:4 and Ephesians 1:10
He will be born in Bethlehem	Micah 5:2	Matthew 2:1 and Luke 2:4-7
The Messiah will return to Jerusalem upon a donkey	Zechariah 9:9	Matthew 21:1-11
He will be sold for 30 pieces of silver	Zechariah 11:12,13	Matthew 26:15 with Matthew 27:3-10
The disciples will forsake him	Zechariah 13:7	Matthew 26:31,56

He will authoritatively return to the temple	Malachi 3:1	Matthew 21:12 and Luke 19:45

It should shock us that more theologians and preachers do not stress these prophecies. Frequently, they are mentioned as a footnote at the end of a sermon. Or, after a mediocre study of the divinity of Christ, a pastor might say, ". . . and there are also a lot of prophecies that show us who Jesus was." No! The prophecies are not a footnote; they are the main event. It is the belief of many theologians that a truth seeker who understands the levity of the messianic prophecies could forget the arguments over creation, false doctrine and the inerrancy of the Bible because the prophecies are the definitive answer to all of these questions.

Traveling in Israel two years before the writing of this book, I had the opportunity to witness to several Jewish men and women of all ages. I remember one night on the coast of the Sea of Galilee in a town called Tiberius, there was a knock on my door at 2:00 am in the morning. Scared for my life, I jumped out of bed, grabbed a lamp from the table ready to do battle with whoever was disturbing my precious slumber. As I opened the door, I found that it wasn't a threat at all; it was a teenager from our church who had opted to come with us at the last minute. With red hair and a boyish smile, he couldn't have looked less menacing. Josh had been excited about theology for months now, and I was always glad to see his face. However, in the middle of the night on the backside of the world when I was trying to steal a few hours of sleep, I could have easily slammed the door, gone back to bed and told my wife that it was an ambitious Jehovah's Witness. "Don't get mad, Brother B," were the first words out of his mouth. Josh couldn't wait to tell me about the encounter he had just had in the hotel lobby where he had very nearly convinced a Jewish girl to give her life to Christ. How did he do it? Surely, he told her she must not ask questions but, rather, take it on faith. Perhaps he encouraged her that the theory of evolution was a farce. Better yet, he probably showed her the Roman road of salvation which always does the trick.

Wrong! Josh had showed her some of the prophecies about the coming Messiah and how they were undeniable. Best of all was that these were verses from the Old Testament that she knew very well from her childhood in an orthodox Jewish home. As he shared the truth of God's Word to her, something clicked. Although she wasn't saved that night, the young lady had more than just a seed planted. She also had more than just a few of Paul's writings shoved down her throat. Out of all the doctors, lawyers, pastors and theologians on that trip, a 17-year-old boy had connected with her culture and changed her heart. And he did it not by thumping Bibles, but with love.

In fact, almost every time a Jewish person is converted, it was in part because they came to a realization that the prophecies were referring to Jesus. Because of this, many preachers have said, "Well, the prophecies are for the Jews." God forbid! The prophecies are just as convincing to anyone who is willing to consider them with an earnest heart.

So convincing are these messianic prophecies that I could end this book right now. The answers are here. Moreover, I could have written only this chapter and the argument for the existence of the Christian God would be just as strong.

I challenge you! Prove these predictions false. It cannot be done. Centuries of philosophers and historians have attempted to discredit Christ via the destruction of the supposed messianic prophecies. The only success that was ever gained in this fruitless endeavor was the logical argument that the exactness of the predictions could only have resulted from the addition of them after the events occurred. This argument prevailed in casting doubt on the prophecies prior to the discovery of the scrolls. Since that time, no one of any profession has had an appropriate answer and thus the fulfillment of the prophecies is, in my opinion, the greatest proof you will find in this or any other book not only for the existence of God but also the Christian God. This blinding light burns as bright as any evidence you will witness.

Chapter 7: His Claims, Influence and Sanity

"I am trying here to prevent anyone saying the really foolish thing that people often say about Him: 'I'm ready to accept Jesus as a great moral teacher, but I don't accept His claim to be God.' That is one thing we must not say. A man who was merely a man and said the sort of thing Jesus said would not be a great moral teacher. He would either be a lunatic—on a level with the man who says he is a poached egg—or else he would be the Devil of Hell. You must make your choice. Either this man was, and is, the Son of God: or else a madman or something worse. You can shut Him up for a fool, you can spit at Him and kill him as a demon or you can fall at his feet and call Him Lord and God. But let us not come with any patronizing nonsense about His being a great human teacher. He has not left that open to us. He did not intend to."- C. S. Lewis[1]

Jesus made an outstanding claim. He said he was God. This was not a claim that others had not made, nor one that men have not made since. Strangely enough, the Old Testament made it clear that a messiah was coming who would fulfill many exact prophecies, but because of the law against blasphemy, when the messiah came preaching of his divinity, he was killed. The Jewish leaders of the time were so content with the system they had firmly in place, they willfully disbelieved his claims of divinity. Not much has changed.

Today, many cults and false doctrines (to be discussed in the next section) deny that Jesus ever claimed to be God. However, the vast majority of Christianity holds to a divine Christ for a reason. In John 10:30, Jesus makes the statement, "***I and my father are one.***" Jehovah's Witnesses will tell you that this was clearly not a claim to godhood but rather an allusion to the fact that Jesus had become like God the father. A weathered old man from the kingdom hall once stood on my porch and showed me a picture of his brother. He asked, "Have you ever seen this man before?" I said, "No sir."

He responded, "You have seen me and my brother--looks a lot like me doesn't he?"

I said, "I guess."

With a clap of the hands he grinned ear to ear and said, "See, there you have it. I and my brother are one and Jesus and God are one." Wait a minute!

Are you as confused by that Jehovah's Witness as I am?

If Jesus did not intend to make the claim that he was God in this statement, why in the world did the Pharisees react by picking up stones to throw at him and accusing him of blasphemy as they did. I suppose the Jehovah's Witnesses with their malformed Bible and deranged founder are able to understand what Jesus was saying better than those who heard it with their own ears. But the conversation did not end there.

As three more Jehovah's witnesses unloaded from the car (the cavalry) and made their way to my porch, I asked about another verse. John 1:1: "***In the beginning was the Word and the Word was with God and the Word was God.***" Verse 14 "***and the Word became flesh and dwelt among us.***" This verse should put the nail in the coffin. Jesus might as well have worn a name tag that said, "Hey, I really am God!" What did the JWs say? They claimed that our translations of the Bible were distorted from the true word of God (the New World Translation). By the way, the NWT is not accepted as credible by anyone outside the Kingdom Hall. No one really knows who the authors were, and much of it was based on a couple of manuscripts rather than the thousands of other translations that lend credibility to other versions. Neither Jesus, nor his hearers were confused about his claims.

Moreover, Jesus' claims to Godhood do not end there. In John 8:56 he claimed, "***Your father Abraham rejoiced to see my day; and he saw it, and was glad***." Verse 58 goes on to say, "***before Abraham was, I AM***." The phrase "***I AM***" was one the Hebrews knew to be indicative of God alone. The Kingdom Hall may not recognize this phrase (it would require actual study) but the Jews certainly did.

So, couldn't he have just lied about being God? Absolutely. But to believe that, one would have to say the miracles were false and Jesus was insane. One of the greatest proofs that Christ was who he said he was can be found in his miracles that testify to him. I was recently standing outside the Nashville Public Library when I noticed a Christian Science reading room (always good for a debate). I walked inside and was confronted by a loving, sincere elderly lady who explained her personal experience with me. I would have been touched if I believed an ounce of what she said was of God. She explained to me that Christian Science holds that the miracles spoken of in the Bible were remarkable but have purely naturalistic explanations. She also held that Jesus never claimed to be God. Finally, I asked her, "If the miracles are not supernatural and Jesus never claimed to be God, then why did Thomas respond, '***My Lord and My God!***' upon seeing the resurrected Lord." She then asked me to leave because I was disturbing her faith.

If the miracles of the Bible were not the incredible feats that they were asserted to be by the authors, then the only explanation is that Jesus brainwashed the crowd. Thousands of people witnessed the miracles of Jesus and became his followers. Perhaps Jesus tricked the crowd and made them believe he was God.

There are a great many problems with this line of thought, not the least of which is that it is incredibly condescending to the followers of Jesus. Think of what you are saying! Five thousand people sitting on a hillside listening to Jesus preach, hear his message and are tricked. In fact, not only are they tricked but they are so brainwashed by this common Jewish man that they think they are eating fish and loaves. What single crowed of 5,000 people could be so brainwashed? "Well," you might say, "The followers of Christ were downtrodden people who lacked the common mental faculties of others. Thus they were easy to trick."

True, some of Christ's followers were afflicted people, but their affliction or poverty has nothing to do with their IQ. Furthermore, Jesus had followers of every walk of life even during his own life time. Roman soldiers, tax collectors, lawyers and even Jewish rulers (Nicodemus) were among his ranks.

How could this many men be so duped by Jesus that they imagined the miracles?

A second argument is that Jesus hypnotized the crowds and forced them to believe he had performed great miracles. Primarily, this should hold no water simply because it is an argument out of desperation rather than an argument which can be ascribed to logic. Adherents of the "hypnotized disciples" philosophy cannot back up their claims with a single instance in history when large groups of people have ever been hypnotized. It takes as much faith to believe in that sort of thing as it does to believe in the miracles. Fortunately, today's leading psychologists have concluded that mass hypnotism is simply not possible.

Maybe Jesus was out of his mind when he claimed that he was God. Certainly we are not at a loss of lunatics throughout history who have made such a claim, but good psychology doesn't show this. First of all, Jesus had countless eyewitnesses to his miracles. If the miracles were false, Jesus would have been insane. But thousands of people saw and testified to his unbelievable power. Moreover, Jesus displayed no signs of insanity. He had no anger. Even at the turning of tables, there was a time of consideration and planning before he proceeded. He had no desire for great power. Surely, he wanted people to serve him, but even his disciples were angered that he did not come to establish an earthly kingdom. Besides, many times he finished his miracles by telling people to remain quiet about what they had seen. Finally, his message was one of peace. He did not encourage mass suicide, sexual orgies, holy homicide or hatred of any person. Psychologist today would conclude that Jesus was a sane man.

So if he claimed to be God, was sane and performed miracles that were witnessed by thousands, we must conclude that he was who he claimed to be. I realize that the most obvious objection to this argument is that much of what we know of Jesus is based on scripture which is, of course, not accepted as factual by many reading this book. However, in the following chapter, we will discuss (among other things) the reasons why the eyewitness accounts of Jesus in the New Testament can be accepted as historical beyond a reasonable doubt.

Consider what we have shown in this chapter. If Jesus was not brainwashing, hypnotizing or tricking anyone, was a sane man, claimed to be God, performed miracles, yet sought no personal glory, the only logical conclusion is that he was who he claimed to be. However, let's imagine that the critics are right, and Jesus was somehow able to hypnotize the crowd or brainwash them into believing he had performed miracles. The question that then surfaces is one of motive. Why would Jesus go to such great lengths only to seek no personal gain? Conversely, he knew that these actions would lead him to die a grizzly death. We can only conclude one of two things about such a person. Either he was God, or he was insane, but as we've shown above, there is no reason to believe him to be crazy. Actually, the kinds of attributes Jesus portrayed show him to be a very well-balanced person.

He Was Not From This World

As I walked down the street in Jacksonville, Florida, one day, I remember seeing a man waving his arms around wildly. As a typical rubberneck, I wanted to see what all the commotion was about. Rushing over, I found that it was simply some fanatic waving a sign that read, "Jesus was a space alien." He was being mocked by the crowed that stood by and laughed.

Silly as this sounds, the man was right . . . sort of. Jesus is alien to this world. He became a human to atone for the sin of man but aside from his human body, he was from another world-- one that we will soon inhabit. So different was he that he stands out in history more than any other leader, king, president, potentate, shaman or monk. Jesus was just different. Forget whether you believe in scripture or not, Jesus has a bigger following than anyone else in the history of the world. Granted, it is considered weak to argue for some thing or ideology based on the number of people that believe in it. After all, at one time, most people thought the world was flat. Still, you've got to admit that there is something strange about one man having such an impact. Entire nations have set Christianity as their fundamental outline for life and legality. This is the case in the Bahamas where racial problems are almost nonexistent, pornography is nowhere to be found and the family unit is as strong as one could hope. In fact, I was told by several men and women there that if you don't believe in God, you'll want to keep that to yourself because people will think there is surely something wrong with you mentally. Wow! That is the opposite of American thinking today.

So what? What difference does it make if Jesus has that kind of following if it doesn't make a positive difference? Jesus made such a mark on planet earth that belief in him is still changing people for the better as no drug; counselor or psychology is able to do. No reference for this is needed. Almost everyone knows someone who has altered their way of living because they have converted to a Christian lifestyle.

At a recent evangelistic meeting near Jackson, Tennessee, a man wandered through the door with no intention of enjoying the service. He had come on invitation from his son who was active in the youth group. When he entered the auditorium, the pastor was shocked. Usually, the fellow wanted to be as far away from church folks as a person can be living in the Bible belt. He owned a liquor store and vowed that he would never become a Christian, because if he did, God might make him stop selling the stuff. At the end of the service, the drawing of God was so strong on the man's life that he pushed aside his selfishness and fell before God. The next day he told the preacher, "I was saved last night." The preacher said, "Really?" The man said, "That's right and today I got rid of my liquor store. Christians can't be selling that mess."

On Easter of 2004, I was pastoring Cornerstone Baptist Church in McMinnville, Tennessee. I was preaching to a packed house. Hundreds of people had turned out. Everyone seems to show up on Easter, don't they? I prepared to preach a message titled "Jesus Is The Only Way." Just before I stood up to preach, I was approached by someone who said, "You better not preach that today."

I said, "Why not?"

They said, "Because Richard is here. And if you preach that way, he'll give you a bloody nose. He hates preachers, and if you say that Jesus is the only way he'll come down that aisle and deck you."

I said, "Well, I guess I better change my message."

A few moments later I stood up to preach and I said, "This morning I would like to preach about Jesus, the only way."

At the end of that service, God moved like never before at Cornerstone. People were committing their lives to Christ all over the auditorium. Finally, I saw Richard coming down the aisle. I knew it was him because he looked just as mean as I had heard. Now I've felt a lot of emotions standing at the altar during an invitation. I had felt concern, and I had felt compassion, but I had never been scared before. I covered my nose and said, "At least let me get ready for it."

Then he threw his arms around my neck. I said, "Why did you come down this aisle?"

He said, "I came to be saved!"

I said, "Are you sure you want to do that?" That day Richard was born again and his life changed. It was a lasting change. In 2005, Cornerstone took a mission trip to Arizona to witness to native-Americans. Richard went along. A couple of days into the experience, he was troubled because he wasn't able to lead anybody to Jesus. Richard is a resourceful man, and he was relentless in looking for a solution to the problem. He bought every jump rope he could get his hands on. Strange as it sounds, he stood in the parking lot of a grocery store and handed out jump ropes to anyone who would let him share Christ with them. Thirty-three people were born again because of Richard.

The testimony of a changed life is hard to deny. Explain to me how a Jewish carpenter who died 2000 years ago could convince a hardened sinner in 2006 to sell his liquor business, and I'll become an atheist. Show me anyone else besides Christ who could inspire a man with the kind of reputation Richard had to become a loving, gentle servant who would travel to the other side of the nation just to stand in a parking lot and preach. We serve a living God who is able to do the unthinkable. Even non-believers have a strange reverence for him.

One of my dearest friends from high school is now an avowed homosexual. He grew up in a conservative Christian home with conservative Christian parents. He attended a conservative church and his school was a conservative Christian one. Today, he has no use for Christianity or even a sense of God. One night as we were sitting around visiting, I asked him if he believed in Jesus. He said, "No." I then asked him if he could simply say, "I don't love Jesus." He said, "I can't say that." I asked him why he was having trouble denying that he loved someone who doesn't even exist and he couldn't tell me. He said, "It just doesn't feel right." I then asked him if he could deny that Jesus was God. Strangely, he could deny that there was a God at all, but had a problem with denying that Jesus was God. For some unknown reason he couldn't deny Christ.

In varying degrees, other unbelievers have trouble showing much disrespect to the Lord. Some are able to deny that he is God. However, many find it difficult to treat him any way but kingly. I submit to you that even those who are not his followers know in their heart who he is. Like a fugitive, they know who pursues them. They have run from him all their lives.

[1]Lewis, C.S. ***Mere Christianity.*** Harper.

[2]Exact source unknown-widely accepted medical description

Chapter 8: His Death, Burial And Resurrection

When Bill Clinton was in office, I often thought, "This man could walk out onto the front lawn of the White House, shoot an innocent bystander, talk about it on CNN that night, and some people would still think he was a savior." It seems as though he was able to get away with just about anything. The opposite seems to be true about Jesus. No matter how much evidence is mounted for his divinity, or how powerful his message of love, there are a vast number of people who have decided ahead of time that they will not accept the idea that Jesus is God. My request of you for the remainder of this chapter is that you would open your mind to the possibility that he is who he claimed to be.

Would you agree with me that if it could be proven beyond a reasonable doubt that Jesus died, was buried and rose again on the third day and after that ascended to heaven, that it would mean he is God? You might say this is impossible. However, I believe that if you were to examine the evidence with the mind of a juror witnessing a trial, you would have to conclude that Jesus is God beyond a reasonable doubt. How can this be done?

His Death

Surprisingly, when critics seek to discredit Christ they seldom begin in the most obvious place. Rather than scrutinizing his resurrection, they often begin by questioning whether he ever really died. The argument is like this: (1) He had to die to rise from the dead; (2) He never really died; (3) So there was no resurrection. The idea is known as the swoon theory. After all that Jesus endured leading up to the crucifixion and the hours spent hanging on the tree, some claim that Jesus merely "swooned" on the cross. That is to say that he didn't really die. He simply feigned death or perhaps lost consciousness from blood loss. But important to this theory is the understanding that he never really died. The soldiers thought he was dead even as did the Jews, but his disciples later revived him and then after a short time he began to reveal himself to others, giving the appearance of resurrection. There are several problems with this idea. First, the critics who follow the swoon theory completely ignore the history of the Romans. These men were professional killers. Making an art out of ending peoples' lives, these monsters were so brutal in their execution that the thought of a man surviving is ludicrous. Added to the crucifixion was the scourging.

"The Roman legionnaire steps forward with the flagrum (or flagellum) in his hand. This is a short whip consisting of several heavy, leather thongs with two small balls of lead attached near the ends of each. The heavy whip was brought down with full force again and again across Jesus' shoulders, back and legs. At first, the thongs cut through the skin only. Then, as the blows continue, they cut deeper into the subcutaneous tissues, producing first an oozing of blood from the capillaries and veins of the skin, and finally spurting arterial bleeding from vessels in the underlying muscles. The small balls of lead first produce large, deep bruises which are broken open by subsequent blows. Finally the skin of the back is hanging in long ribbons and the entire area is an unrecognizable mass of torn, bleeding tissue. When it is determined by the centurion in charge that the prisoner is near death, the beating is finally stopped."[2]

Clearly, a man could not survive after the scourging for very long. If Jesus had been released after this bloody mess, he still wouldn't have survived. Furthermore, when you consider that this was only the beginning, it becomes clear how brutal the ordeal was. Next came the crucifixion.

What is crucifixion? "A medical doctor provides a physical description. The cross is placed on the ground and the exhausted man is quickly thrown backwards with his shoulders against the wood. The legionnaire feels for the depression at the front of the wrist. He drives a heavy, square wrought-iron nail through the wrist and deep into the wood. Quickly he moves to the other side and repeats the action, being careful not to pull the arms too tightly but to allow some flex and movement. The cross is then lifted into place.

The left foot is pressed backward against the right foot, and with both feet extended, toes down, a nail is driven through the arch of each, leaving the knees flexed. The victim is now crucified. As he slowly sags down with more weight on the nails in the wrists, excruciating, fiery pain shoots along the fingers and up the arms to explode in the brain-- the nails in the wrists are putting pressure on the median nerves. As he pushes himself upward to avoid this stretching torment, he places the full weight on the nail through his feet. Again he feels the searing agony of the nail tearing through the nerves between the bones of his feet. As the arms fatigue, cramps sweep through the muscles, knotting them in deep, relentless, throbbing pain. With these cramps comes the inability to push himself upward to breathe. Air can be drawn into the lungs but not exhaled. He fights to raise himself in order to get even one small breath. Finally, carbon dioxide builds up in the lungs and in the blood stream, and the cramps partially subside. Spasmodically, he is able to push himself upward to exhale and bring in life-giving oxygen.

Hours of this limitless pain include cycles of twisting, joint-rending cramps, intermittent partial asphyxiation, and searing pain as tissue is torn from his lacerated back when he moves up and down against the rough timber. Then another agony begins-- a deep, crushing pain deep in the chest as the pericardium slowly fills with serum and begins to compress the heart. It is now almost over--the loss of tissue fluids has reached a critical level--the compressed heart is struggling to pump heavy, thick, sluggish blood into the tissues--the tortured lungs are making a frantic effort to gasp in small gulps of air. He can feel the chill of death creeping through his tissues. . .finally, he can allow his body to die.

All this the Bible records with the simple words, "***And they crucified Him***." (Mark 15:24). What wondrous love is this?"[2]

Can you imagine a man living through such a thing, particularly without the medical help that we have in the modern world? And remember, there isn't much debate about the fact that a man named Jesus claiming to be God was crucified by the Romans. Yet, somehow the question is whether he really died. The Roman legions would roar with laughter at hearing such a ridiculous argument as the swoon theory. Or, perhaps they would be offended.

As already mentioned, a Roman executioner was familiar with death. It would be an insult to say of him that he was mistaken about Jesus' death. Moreover, Roman military law reveals that if a man was given the responsibility of killing someone, and the man was found living, then the soldier himself would face extreme punishment and possibly death. After seeing this evidence, I sincerely hope it is impossible for you to believe that Christ somehow swooned on the cross. He died.

His Burial

"When the even was come, there came a rich man of Arimathaea, named Joseph, who also himself was Jesus' disciple: He went to Pilate, and begged the body of Jesus. Then Pilate commanded the body to be delivered. And when Joseph had taken the body, he wrapped it in a clean linen cloth, And laid it in his own new tomb, which he had hewn out in the rock: and he rolled a great stone

to the door of the sepulchre, and departed."
– Matthew 27:57-60

How true is the record of the burial found in the Bible? First, it should be recognized that there has not been much argument throughout history about whether or not Jesus was indeed buried. Most would agree that this is the case. Vastly, the argument against Jesus divinity focuses on the death and resurrection. Still, it is needful for us to understand a couple of simple facts about the burial of Christ.

Understanding the location of the tomb of Jesus is helpful in establishing an argument of credibility. In modern day Jerusalem, there are at least two possible locations for the tomb. Church history is divided on this issue. The church of the Holy Sepulcher in the old city of Jerusalem was placed there by Constantine as a memorial and to preserve the location of the tomb. Remember, prior to the conversion of Constantine, there was great persecution for the church, and thus the location of the tomb, if known, would have been kept a secret. Roman soldiers would have happily desecrated this place in order to break down the morale of the budding church. For this reason, it is greatly suspected that Constantine merely chose a location that was acceptable. Moreover, though many theologians demand that this must be the location of the tomb, it is seemingly too close to the city. Granted, Jerusalem has grown, and at the time of the crucifixion the spot was outside the city walls. But it was just outside. This seems too close to the city for many historians. Outlandishly, the church not only contains the supposed tomb but also the very spot of the crucifixion. Indeed, scripture indicates that these two sites were not far apart, but come on. Adherents would almost have us believe that Jesus just fell off the cross and into the tomb. Finally, in criticizing this location, there is much competition among Christian groups to claim the location as their own "holy spot." At least three groups, "the Greek Orthodox, Anglicans and, of course, Roman Catholic churches all share the structure built around the site. Believe it or not, at one point in the church there is a line on the floor, dividing the Greek Orthodox section from that of the Roman Catholic. Furthermore, there are even special moments that have been fabricated for the very purpose of claiming ownership. By this I mean one of the three churches built a gazebo style structure only sixteen square-feet large right in the middle of the church, claiming that it is holy because Mary stood there and cried. Does it not seem that there is a lot of mischief going on in the church?

The second (and in my opinion more acceptable) site is located just a few miles from the old city of

Jerusalem in a lush garden near a hill strangely resembling a skull. The Bible calls the hill of Christ's death Golgotha. In the Greek the word is **Kranion,** meaning "skull." The site now referred to as "the garden tomb" was discovered in 1881 when Charles Gordon began researching the hill. For this reason, some refer to it as "Gordon's Calvary." As he studied, he became aware of a tomb that had recently been uncovered, meeting the exact qualifications the biblical record gives. Moreover, there were even discovered etchings on the outside of the tomb which indicated that early Christians worshipped there. The strength of this site is in its biblical validity. The four gospel writers make several things clear about the location of the tomb. Primarily, John claimed that Christ's tomb was in a garden. Mark is even more specific:

> *"And when they looked, they saw that the stone was rolled away: for it was very great. And entering into the sepulchre, they saw a young man sitting on the right side, clothed in a long white garment; and they were affrighted."* – *Mark 16:4,5*

Notice that Mark claims the man was sitting on the right side. Understanding the design of most tombs of the day, one can see that this would mean the tomb had an entrance and a spot to stand which was just to the left of the spot where the body would lie. Interestingly, tombs were usually situated so that the body was placed to the left of the door. In this case it is the reverse. This is highly uncommon and lends credence to Gordon's location.

Whichever site is correct, the point is still made. For our purposes, we must understand that modern archaeological discoveries and early Christian traditions have pointed us to one of two probable locations where Jesus was buried and is absent, but (this is the kicker) after constant archaeological digging in a relatively small geographic location, critics have not been able to produce a single tomb containing the remains of Jesus. The task should be relatively simple. This combined with the fact that even the critics of the day never questioned that Jesus was buried should lead us to the logical conclusion that Jesus was entombed and that his body no longer resides therein.

Since I originally drafted this chapter a great controversy over an archaeological discovery in Israel has been manifested. The supposed remains of Christ were brought to light resting in a burial container in Jerusalem. Because of this it is needful to make a couple of comments on the subject. There are several reasons to doubt the veracity of the claim that this box actually contains Christ's remains. (1) The box was not discovered recently, but in the 1980's. It is not a new discovery. (2) It didn't receive much credit from archaeologists in the 80's and since the buzz about it recently died after the first week it is clear that no credit will be given now either. (3) The names mentioned on the box (Mary, Joseph and Jesus) were common names. In this regard it is similar to looking at a cemetery in Mexico where you will find countless tombstones with the names Mary, Joseph and Jesus on them. (4) Carbon dating of the box gives varied results. (5) At present it has become all the rage to cast doubt on the historical reliability of the Bible (to be dealt with in the following chapter). The fictional works of Dan Brown, the new emphasis put on the Gospel of Judas (dated to at least 200 years after Judas), the gospel of Mary Magdalene and the extremely biased work of the Jesus Seminar have all shown that non-Christian America has been screaming for an archaeological discovery like this. (6) James Cameron is its biggest advocate. No group of respected scholars today gives serious credence to this find.

THE RESURRECTION

*"**Moreover, brethren, I declare unto you the gospel which I preached unto you, which also ye have received, and wherein ye stand; By which also ye are saved, if ye keep in memory what I preached unto you, unless ye***

have believed in vain. For I delivered unto you first of all that which I also received, how that Christ died for our sins according to the scriptures; And that he was buried, and that he rose again the third day according to the scriptures" 1 Corinthians 15:1-4

Paul made an outrageous claim about Jesus. He claimed that Jesus rose again. So far, we have demonstrated beyond a reasonable doubt that Jesus died, was buried and was later removed somehow from the tomb. I want to say again: if it can be shown that Jesus rose from death to life beyond a reasonable doubt then it should be accepted that he is God. How can this be proven? Don't be turned off when I say that I am going to use the Bible itself to make this argument. I realize that it is bad logic to use a thing to prove that same thing. Although in this case the eyewitness testimonies of Christ's resurrection are airtight and logically defensible. Moreover, the passage of scripture mentioned above is accepted by even the liberal anti-religious "Jesus Seminar" as authentic and true.

Paul has claimed in the above passage that Jesus died, was buried and rose from the grave. Imagine that the same thing was claimed about the president. What if it was stated that the president died, was buried and rose again? We would all think this was foolishness. But what if we found over 500 people who all testified to the fact that he truly did what is being claimed--not liberals, by the way, but logical and honest people. What if they all stood in a courtroom and gave the same report about the same event, though they were scattered all over the country and did not correspond. Say what you like, but the argument would be hard to beat. This is exactly what is represented in Paul's argument.

> *"And that he was seen of Cephas, then of the twelve: After that, he was seen of above five hundred brethren at once; of whom the greater part remain unto this present, but some are fallen asleep. After that, he was seen of James; then of all the apostles. And last of all he was seen of me also, as of one born out of due time." 1 Corinthians 15:5-8*

Paul said that Jesus was seen after his resurrection alive and well. He wasn't seen by ten, fifty or one hundred. Jesus was seen in several different locations by over five hundred people who were all willing to testify to the event. Once again, I realize that some might say, "How do we know that Paul did not make this up?" This is a good question and deserves a logical response.

Paul claimed in this passage that most of those who saw the risen Christ were still living at the time he wrote to the Corinthians. This scripture was duplicated literally hundreds if not thousands of times. We know this because of the number of 1 Corinthians manuscripts discovered all over the world. Now think. If Paul lied in a claim that was duplicated world wide, mentioned specific names of people who saw the risen Lord, and that in one outstanding sociological event Christ revealed himself to 500 people, shouldn't there be someone who refuted this. Indeed, wouldn't the government that was so opposed to Christianity find Israelites who would deny that a gathering of 500 ever claimed to have seen such a thing? Wouldn't those whose names Paul mentioned speak out against him? Of the countless manuscripts that support Paul's claims, not one single manuscript has ever been located anywhere in the world at any time stating that what Paul said was untrue.

Someone might claim, "Well, by the time Paul's letter to the Corinthians was circulated and reproduced those critics would be dead." Not so! This was a world in which verbal communication and written dialogue was paramount to a successful society. Historical records show that things taking place in Israel were heard about in Rome within a few days. Moreover, the Hebrews are known for their verbal history. Even today, Hebrew families pass on what they know of history from one generation to the next with virtually no discrepancies. American men tell their kids they caught a catfish that weighed fifteen pounds and three weeks later it is reported that a catfish the size of a Volkswagen was pulled out of the lake. The Hebrews are not like this. They are exact. Even if it could be said that the original critics were dead by the time Paul's letter had gained popularity, the offspring of those critics would have set the record straight.

Lee Strobel, in his book, *The Case for Christ*, explains that the testimony of this many witnesses would be an insurmountable case that the event was true. If each was given just fifteen minutes to give testimony and the court took no recess, it would take at least an entire week to hear each argument. Any jury would love to have that kind of assurance. It is pretty clear that Christ rose again beyond a reasonable doubt. However, there is more evidence.

Perhaps the strongest argument for the validity of the resurrection is the truth that men will not die for a lie. Historical records like, "The Works of Josephus," claim that each of the apostles died a martyr's death for preaching the resurrection of Christ with the exception of John who was boiled in oil and then banished to Patmos. The only group who would have benefited from hiding the body of Christ would have been the apostles. The Jewish leaders and the Romans both wanted an end to the chaos surrounding the life and death of Jesus of Nazareth. So the question remains, "Why would these men all die for something they knew to be untrue?" Men will live for a lie, but they will not die for one under any circumstances. Remember, these men were all from different walks of life and it is prohibitively unlikely that they were brainwashed. Moreover, even if they were lunatics, the fact remains that they would have seen the dead Christ. Produce one man in history who has ever died for something he knew to be untrue for no recognizable reason and you will have an argument. Some would site the suicide bombers of extremist Muslims, but extremist Muslims truly believe in what they are dieing for. Others might site lunatics like Jim Jones, but remember these cultic leaders are lunatics. The apostles would have known that they were dieing for a lie, and men just don't do that.

Thus, we may conclude from this chapter that the death, burial and resurrection of Jesus of Nazareth were all authentic events and logically defensible. Following these arguments to their end gives undeniable proof to the statement "Paul's claims about Christ are true beyond a reasonable doubt."

Chapter 9: The Trustworthiness Of The Bible

Because Jesus is the central figure of the Bible, duty demands that we discuss the veracity of this collection of books. For that reason, this chapter will be a discussion without much illustration on the validity of scripture. It is my intent to remove all reasonable doubt from the mind of the reader regarding the trustworthiness of the Bible. The myth that the Bible is only a religious book is simply illogical when the glaring evidences of its authenticity are discovered. This is one of the most powerful blinding lights that will be discussed; the glaring evidences for biblical truth.

We have established beyond a reasonable doubt that there is a God. He is the cause of the universe and exists outside of time, space and matter. This is not a religious belief; it is the deduction of the scientific laws accepted by all. Next, we established that Jesus is God. The eyewitness testimonies and historical facts surrounding the life of Jesus in conjunction with the undeniable prophecies about the coming messiah bring us to the point that we may also say his claims to Godhood have been proven beyond a reasonable doubt. Knowing these things to be true, it would seem clear to us that a personal loving God would have attempted to communicate with his creation. Any opposing view is almost prohibited when considering the implications of the moral, ethical, personal and loving God described by C.S. Lewis. Remember, Lewis made his argument based on findings outside of the Bible.

So, how would God communicate with man? The most obvious way would be to use the common means of communication of which man is aware-- written language. We could expect that God would communicate in this way. It is logical, and we serve a logical God. The problem, then, is finding the right religious writing. Indeed, there are a multitude of books on the subject that should be considered. Primarily, there are three collections of scripture that are accepted among large groups of people today-- that of the Jews, the Christians and the Muslims. The Jewish Bible is contained in the Christian Old Testament, and for this reason the only opposing scripture that it would be needful for us to discuss is that of the Muslims.

The Qur'an is illogical. It has become very popular since September 11, 2001, to be a Muslim. "Islam is a peaceful religion," we are often told. The support for these ignorant claims is a contextual one. It is asserted by the Qur'an's defenders that if we read the violent passages of the Qur'an in the right context, we will find new meaning that is more peaceful than Christianity. Really? Actually, the Qur'an has no context. It is arranged based on length of chapter rather than chronology of thought. Thus, finding the actual meaning of a passage is a fruitless endeavor. Moreover, the god of the Qur'an is in stark contrast to the God revealed by general revelation (what we see in nature). Trusting this document is also dangerous because of the way it was received by Mohammed. M. H. Haykal, a Muslim biographer wrote, "Stricken with fear Muhammad arose and asked himself, 'what did I see? Did possession of the Devil which I feared all along come to pass? Muhammad looked to his right and his left but saw nothing. For a while he stood there stricken with fear and trembling with awe. He feared that the cave might be haunted and that he might run away still unable to explain what he saw." Clearly, even the great prophet of the Muslims was a very confused guy.

An entire book could be written on the inconsistencies present in the Qur'an, but the purpose of our endeavor does not warrant it. Much could be said of Muhammad's inability to perform miracles to demonstrate his authenticity even though he admitted that previous prophets had. Dozens of things contained in the Qur'an are in stark contrast to science. Archaeology discredits the Qur'an regularly while upholding biblical history.

However, it will be more productive for us not to discredit the Qur'an but rather credit the Bible. The purpose, then, of having discussed these three primary texts is simply to find a logical scripture to consider. Whether the Christian Bible is the Word of God remains to be seen.

How can we trust the Bible? Strange as it may sound, the best place to begin is in the New Testament. Think about it. If it can be made sure that the New Testament is a true account, it will follow that what Jesus said about the Old Testament will present itself as honest. What do we know factually about the New Testament?

At present there are documented at least 24,000 handwritten copies of the New Testament and more being discovered by archaeologists every day. A few of those copies date to within one generation of their author. Homer's Iliad is second in line behind the New Testament in terms of number of copies to back it up with only 643 manuscripts-- still its authorship, date and historical (non-fictional) claims are not debated. Yet, somehow we debate the validity of an entirely non-fictional work written by many authors with 24,000 copies to verify its truthfulness. Some might argue that there are inconsistencies or discrepancies between these 24,000 copies and they would be right. Often these minor differences are held up as absolute proof that the Bible is a fraud. Over 155,000 differences exist between these 24,000 copies, and even though that sounds like a lot, it isn't. One copy might refer to the Lord as "Jesus of Nazareth," while another refers to him as "Jesus Christ," or yet another might simply say, "Jesus." Furthermore, out of all those copies there are only about 50 discrepancies that would make even the smallest theological difference and none that would affect doctrine. Keep in mind, it is very possible to have discrepancies in a document and still understand with exactness what the author meant to say. Imagine that you received a letter that said "Yo#r house is burning!" Would you have any question about what that meant? No. In fact you would call the fire department and rush with great concern to your home. The same could be said if you received the messages, "Your h#use is burning! Or Your house #s burning!" The message is intact in spite of a minor flaw. In all honesty, these tiny mistakes should lend more credit to the Bible's authenticity because it means that the scribes who translated saw the problem but were so bound by duty that they even copied the mistakes. It is amazing how well preserved the documents are.

Many have attempted to explain the striking similarities among these copies by claiming that they had been tampered with. Overzealous monks changed them to look alike. Imagine what that would mean were it true. These monks were so intelligent that they were able to discover 24,000+ copies of the New Testament from all over the world, change them with the ability of a CSI and then place them back in their original locations so perfectly that an archaeologist would never suspect that anyone had been there. If you believe that, you've got more faith than any Christian. We can factually say that the New Testament we've got today (true of false) is the same one that was written nearly two millennia ago. And although our primary consideration at the moment is the New Testament, archaeology backs up the validity of the whole Bible. Listen to what Mark McGee in his article, "Archaeology and the Bible," quotes several archaeologists as saying:

William F. Albright - "There can be no doubt that archaeology has confirmed the substantial historicity of Old Testament traditions." [1]

Miller Burrows - "Archaeology has in many cases refuted the views of modern critics. It has shown in a number of instances that these views rest on false assumptions and unreal, artificial schemes of historical development ... The excessive skepticism of many liberal theologians stems not from a careful evaluation of the available data, but from an enormous predisposition against the supernatural."[1]

F.F. Bruce - "Where Luke has been suspected of inaccuracy, and accuracy has been vindicated by some inscriptional evidence, it may be legitimate to say archaeology has confirmed the New Testament record." [1]

Merrill Unger - "Old Testament archaeology has rediscovered whole nations, resurrected important peoples, and in a most astonishing manner filled in historical gaps, adding immeasurably to the knowledge of biblical backgrounds." [1]

Nelson Glueck - "It may be stated categorically that no archaeological discovery has ever controverted a biblical reference." [1]

Archaeologists admit that not only the New Testament but the entire Bible is in accordance with what we know of history.

HARMONY

The Biblical writers also wrote with an amazing degree of harmony. Most non-biblical scholars cannot explain the degree of accuracy that exists between the various authors. With 44 writers scattered across centuries, a document has been woven together so perfectly that it is consistent both historically and doctrinally. How is this possible? You would almost believe that there was really only one author, God. God's handiwork would also be the only explanation for the prophecies discussed in previous chapters. Abraham's story was written down between 750 and 1200 years prior to Christ and yet it speaks of things that came true while Jesus was alive. Remember when we established that the cause of the universe must have been something that exists outside of space, matter and time. The truth of that third category (time) is clearly seen in the biblical harmony that transcends history.

Obviously, there is an abundance of evidence to support the texts we have of the New Testament today as authentic. Also, most scholars (both Christian and non-Christian) concede that there is a great degree of harmony in the Bible not seen in any other book in history. Finally, with regard to the New Testament, we have already shown that what it has to say about Jesus of Nazareth is true beyond a reasonable doubt. We know that what it says about Hebrew history is true from a multitude of other sources so we are left asking the question, "What is left to be skeptical about?" If we have shown that Jesus was God without relying on the trustworthiness of the Bible and that it is historically accurate in all things political, the only things left to doubt are the miracles. C. S. Lewis wrote a book on miracles (literally). Naturally, it is a fascinating study. However, if we have demonstrated the veracity of the greatest miracle (the resurrection of Jesus) how can we question Christ's ability to perform other, lesser supernatural works?

It has been said that there is greater evidence for the trustworthiness of the New Testament than for the existence of America's first president, George Washington. If a skeptic argues against its validity, we must respond, "Show us the evidence against it. The burden of proof is on you." Indeed, the New Testament is such a sure document that it is more reliable than the morning paper (especially if you read the New York Times). There simply is no logical reason left for doubting the claims of the New Testament.

Knowing that the New Testament is a trustworthy collection, we have built a great foundation for proving the authenticity of the rest of the Bible.

The Old Testament

"And he said unto them, These are the words which I spake unto you, while I was yet with you, that all things must be fulfilled, which were written in the law of Moses, and in the prophets, and in the psalms, concerning me." – Luke 24:44

Christ himself (now a trustworthy New Testament character) speaks here of the validity of three writings (The law of Moses, the prophets and the Psalms.) What are these three writings? They are the three primary divisions of the Old Testament. **The Law of Moses** consists of: Genesis, Exodus, Leviticus, Numbers and Deuteronomy. The **Prophets** are: Joshua, Judges, Ruth, I Samuel, II Samuel, I Kings, II Kings, Isaiah, Jeremiah, Lamentations, Ezekiel, Hosea, Joel, Amos, Obadiah, Jonah, Micah, Nahum, Habakkuk, Zephaniah, Haggai, Zechariah and Malachi. Finally **the Psalms** (or the Writings) are made up of: Psalms, Proverbs, Job, Song of Solomon, Ecclesiastes, Esther, Daniel, Ezra, Nehemiah, I Chronicles and II Chronicles.

We may from this be sure of one thing. Jesus believed in the trustworthiness of the Old Testament. However, one problem still remains. How can we know if the books contained in our copy of the Old Testament are the same ones that the Hebrews had during the time of Christ. A great difficult emerges when we consider that Catholicism, Mormonism and various other faiths include more books than are represented in the protestant Bible. Is there a way to know for sure? Yes!

Flavius Josephus was a Jewish historian living from A.D. 37 to about A.D. 100. Needless to say, he was well aware of all aspects of the religious Jewish life, and certainly what they considered to be scripture. Admittedly some skeptics believe that Christians added to what Josephus wrote, but the following passage is not questioned by scholars. In **Against Apion**, I, 8 He claims:

> *"For we [Jews] have not an innumerable multitude of books among us, disagreeing from and contradicting one another, as the Greeks have, but only twenty-two books, which contain the records of all the past times; which are justly believed to be divine;"*[2]

Now we can know for certain that the Old Testament as it existed in the time of Christ was made up of no more and no less than 22 books. Now it appears that we have a problem. Our Old Testament consists of 39 books. How then can we say that we have the right scripture if numbers don't match? Actually, they match perfectly.

Originally, many of the books in our Old Testament were combined. For example, Judges and Ruth were originally not two books but one. This is true of many of the books in the Old Testament. The original Hebrew scripture thus appeared as follows with the combined books in parenthesis:

The Law of Moses: Genesis, Exodus, Leviticus, Numbers and Deuteronomy.

The Prophets – Former: Joshua, (Judges and Ruth), (I & II Samuel), (I & II Kings)

The Prophets – Latter: Isaiah, (Jeremiah and Lamentations), Ezekiel and (Hosea, Joel, Amos, Obadiah, Jonah, Micah, Nahum, Habakkuk, Zephaniah, Haggai, Zechariah and Malachi all as one book)

The Psalms (or Writings): Psalms, Proverbs, Job, Song of Solomon, Ecclesiastes, Esther, Daniel, (Ezra and Nehemiah) and (I & II Chronicles).

Counting the number of books in the Old Testament with an understanding of these groupings it becomes clear that our 39 books actually condense to 22 just as the Bible of the Hebrews.

These evidences have brought us far. We can now say with certainty that Jesus preached the veracity of the Hebrew Old Testament, that it contained 22 books (just as ours), and that it contained three distinct sections that are the same as ours. However, if all of this still does not convince you that the books of our Old Testament are the same as those to which Jesus referred, consider this statement by the Lord:

> *"From the blood of Abel unto the blood of Zecharias, which perished between the altar and the temple; verily I say unto you, It shall be required of this generation."* – Luke 11:51

It seems certain that Jesus was speaking to the religious leaders about all of the prophets of the Old Testament. Yet, Zecharias is found in Chronicles. Remember that in the Hebrew Bible, as demonstrated above, Chronicles is the last book. Chronologically, Zecharias was the last Old Testament prophet to die. Piling up even more evidence for the truthfulness of the Old Testament, Jesus indicates the very arrangement we have mentioned.

A Changed Life

I would never use this as an evidence for the Bible's authenticity without other evidences, but having seen the undeniable facts that validate God's Word, it should be mentioned that the divinity of the Bible is shown each time a life is changed positively by its teachings. Hardened sinners have been transformed because of God's communication through scripture. They saw the blinding light. Stories of these converts are sprinkled throughout this book, but two are so evident of this truth that they bear mention here.

In their book on Christian child rearing, Meier and Baker tell the story of a man so changed by the Bible that he devoted his life to preserving it:

> "Many years ago in St. Louis, a lawyer visited a Christian to transact some business. Before the two parted, his client said to him, 'I've often wanted to ask you a question, but I've been afraid to do so.' 'What do you want to know?' asked the lawyer. The man replied, 'I've wondered why you're not a Christian.' The man hung his head, 'I know enough about the Bible to realize that it says no drunkard can enter the kingdom of God; and you know my weakness!' 'You're avoiding my questions,' continued the believer. 'Well, truthfully, I can't recall anyone ever explaining how to become a Christian.' Picking up a Bible, the client read some passages showing that all are under condemnation, but that Christ came to save the lost by dying on the cross for their sins. 'By receiving Him as your Substitute and Redeemer,' he said, 'You can be forgiven. If you're willing to receive Jesus, let's

pray together.' The lawyer agreed, and when it was his turn, he exclaimed, 'O Jesus, I am a slave to drink. One of your servants has shown me how to be saved. O God, forgive my sins and help me overcome the power of this terrible habit in my life.' Right there he was converted. That lawyer was C.I. Scofield, who later edited the reference Bible that bears his name. Scofield's Bible is still a favorite among preachers and theologians to this day.[3]

However, others have been converted while attempting to discredit the Bible. Sir Willam Ramsay was so certain that the book of Acts was historically inaccurate that he traveled to the Middle East to prove his hypothesis. After scrutinizing every testable fact of the document, he discovered to his horror that there were fewer flaws in Acts than in most modern day history books. Moved by this, he converted to Christianity and devoted the remainder of his life to defending the inerrancy of the Bible.

1 Copyright ©, **Mark Mcgee** 1990-2000/ *mamcgee@mindspring.com*

2 *The Works of Josephus*

3 Meier, P. **Christian Child Rearing**. Baker.

SECTION 3

Knowing from the first two sections that God exists and Jesus Christ is the Son of God, we have no logical reason left for doubting the validity of the Bible. So weighty is the evidence in the last chapter in conjunction with the prophetic evidences at the start of Section Two, we may conclude that the brilliance of the blinding lights has been proven undeniable yet again. What's left? Actually, we are only at the halfway mark if proving Christian theism is the goal in view. We may agree that Jesus Christ is the Son of God, but to which Jesus are we referring. There are literally hundreds of competing views about who Jesus is. For this reason, Section Three will be a discussion of the many false teachings about Jesus. Among Christian circles this will perhaps be the most controversial section of the book. Still, it is necessary to know what logic and biblical truth have to say about this. Each of the false doctrines to be discussed is representative of a major misunderstanding about Jesus, and so they were not picked out of spite or anger. Moreover, having bridged the gap between general and special revelation, we may now trust the Bible to be the Word of God and the ultimate answer on all detailed spiritual matters.

Chapter 10: Why Discredit False Doctrine

"Jude, the servant of Jesus Christ, and brother of James, to them that are sanctified by God the Father, and preserved in Jesus Christ, and called: Mercy unto you, and peace, and love, be multiplied. Beloved, when I gave all diligence to write unto you of the common salvation, it was needful for me to write unto you, and exhort you that ye should earnestly contend for the faith which was once delivered unto the saints. For there are certain men crept in unawares, who were before of old ordained to this condemnation, ungodly men, turning the grace of our God into lasciviousness, and denying the only Lord God, and our Lord Jesus Christ. –Jude 1:1-4

Have you ever been driving down the road and seen one of those cars in which there is a student driver and a teacher in the seat next to him? Now that's a different kind of education. I mean sitting in the classroom, taking a written test, you might lose a few points for making a mistake. You might get a "B" on that quiz instead of an "A," but out there in that car, if you make a mistake, you're not going to lose a few points; it's serious. Dogs, cats and squirrels could lose their lives. You mess up out there and you could really lose something. When that teacher feels that you are making a mistake, he doesn't correct you in a nice, calm, orderly way. When he sees a blind person crossing the road, he shouts, "WATCH OUT!"

Jude is preaching a message today to you and me, and it is a message that there is trouble coming for Christians everywhere. This message is different from other messages in the Word of God, because this one is urgent, serious and leaves Jude shouting to us, "WATCH OUT!"

There are many things given to us by Christ when we serve him. We receive grace, love, peace, hope, the Holy Spirit and a great many other gifts. But of all of the things that come to us when we serve the Lord Jesus Christ, perhaps the most assuring is faith. Jesus is faithful.

When I was in a college philosophy class, I was sitting next to an atheist and he discovered that I believed in Jesus. He said, "Oh, faith is your answer for everything," and I said, "Well then, what do you believe?"

He said, "I believe that in the beginning a bunch of aliens came in a great space ship and planted an intergalactic seed from their planet and out of it grew what we know today as earth."

I said, "Do you really believe that?"

He said, "Yes."

I thought to myself "Now who has got faith?" Faith in Christ is the only hope for humanity.

Jude is preaching a warning to his students as if a freight train was bearing down upon them. I want to tell you, God put the Bible together the way he did for a reason, and what Jude says to that group of Christians is just as important to modern day believers. The sermon that Jude preaches here is a sermon of emergency. And it's about an emergency in your life.

We Contend For The Faith

I'll tell you if there's a preacher anywhere in the New Testament that was sure enough a Southern Baptist, it's Jude. Jude says, "Listen, I would love to preach to you a wonderful, cute, boring sermon on how wonderful it is to be saved. That's what I came here to do, but there is something more important that we need to talk about. It's time for you to contend for the faith. It's time for you all to fight for this thing." (Paraphrase mine). People like us know how to fight; we just don't fight the right people. We know how to fight. Just think about most churches today.

I've said before that I love the Discovery Channel. I love it. I watch it for the same reason as everyone else. But the more I see it, the more I become convinced that these animals on the Discovery Channel have got to be church members somewhere. One antelope will get too close to another antelope's territory. You've seen it. I mean that's where that antelope likes to sit on Sunday mornings; you had better not come near that spot because that's his spot. But that other antelope keeps pacing around. Finally, that territorial antelope stands from where he's seated and they go at it. There are antlers going everywhere, fur is flying and they get their antlers stuck together, refusing to release. Just about the time you're really getting into their fight and it looks like the final blow is coming, a great big elephant that we didn't know anything about comes along and tramples both of them.

What Jude is doing is giving a warning about that great enemy that is on its way. In fact, it is an enemy that he says is already here. What does he say this enemy is? I've got nothing against Pentecostal and non-denominational churches, but there are a lot of preachers out there who are doing just exactly what Jude is here warning us against, and that's preaching that God is a God of love but not a God of judgment. He'll forgive you of anything so don't feel bad if you're living in sin.

This is what Jude is warning us about--the idea is that God is a God of love and whatever you do is okay with him. There is no punishment for sin. This is why our nation is on a downward spiral. It's why you've got women who can claim to be a Christian but have an abortion. It is why men can sit through an entire church service and then go home and turn on that pornographic movie. God is not seen as a God of judgment.

And by the way, it's time we started calling sin sin. That's what it is. It turns my stomach to hear some parents who just discovered that their child was caught with marijuana, or that their child has been involved sexually, or even that their child was simply caught in a lie, and their response is that that child just made a mistake. Lady, your child didn't just make a mistake; your child committed a grievous sin against God.

I want you to remember that Jesus did not climb on the cross to fix a mistake. He climbed up there to become a sacrifice for sin. In our minds we've got this idea of a happy-go-lucky Jesus. A happy-go-lucky Jesus wouldn't have walked down the path that led to Calvary carrying an old rugged cross. A happy-go-lucky Jesus wouldn't have crawled up on that tree. A happy-go-lucky Jesus wouldn't have hung there for the sin of the world. If that's the Jesus your serving, then you are not serving the Jesus who is. Jesus is a warrior. He is a fighter and a lover.

You might say, "What a horrible way to describe the Lord Jesus." Friend, Jesus said himself, ***"Do not suppose that I have come to bring peace to the earth. I did not come to bring peace, but a sword." - Matthew 10:34*** When Jesus was hanging on the cross, the most important battle of all time was being waged inside the mind and body of our precious Lord as sin fought against righteousness.

I want you to know that we are a people who are soldiers in the army of the Lord, and we had better start fighting his fight for him before America is lost. This is what I'm saying, and I believe it is foolish to think any other way. Right now, the church of Jesus Christ has got a window of only a few more decades, perhaps only a few more years to really fight for the faith before this world truly closes the door on Christ all together. It's time we quit living this mild mannered sort of Christian life and really started doing something to contend.

We Contain The Faith

Jude says that we have been entrusted with this faith. God gave us this faith to take care of it. We don't just contend for no reason; we contend for the faith because we contain the faith.

Several months back I was taking out the garbage. I had several bags and I was going back and forth from the car to a dumpster, and just as I through the last bag into the dumpster and dusted my hands off, I realized that my wedding ring was gone. I thought it must have somehow slipped off my finger as I was throwing the garbage away. Well, I thought about it for a few minutes and finally I climbed up onto the side of that dumpster and looked around in it. Of course I couldn't see a thing. I stepped in with one foot and felt around with my hand. Before I knew it, half of my body was underneath other people's garbage looking for that ring. I didn't find a thing and I sure didn't want to go home and face Sarah. I said, "Lord God, I haven't asked for much in my life, but I'm begging you for something now. God, you have given me salvation in my spirit but God, if I'm going to get salvation in this body, you've got to let me find this thing because Sarah's going to kill me." I had it all planned out I was going to go and buy a replacement and never tell her for the rest of our lives. Still, I wanted to check the house before I left. I got there, slipped by her while still covered in garbage. Then I saw it--sitting by the sink in the bathroom. I don't even remember taking it off. I want to tell you that I had my own private worship service right there at the bathroom sink.

That ring was given to me as a symbol of something. It was entrusted to me and it was my job to take care of it. That ring means a lot to me, but it is not nearly as important as the faith that God entrusted to all of us. As a result, it ought to mean enough to us that we would be willing to crawl through the dirt and the mire and garbage if we have to do that just to protect it. That faith is being attacked. Jude is warning us of men who are claiming to be men of God but are preaching a false gospel. I fear that we have just a short time to get our loved ones into church and before the throne of God. It's time to contend for the faith because this generation of Christianity is buying in to what these false teachers are selling.

Just two nights ago, there was a dear lady in my office and I was counseling her. She was in a desperate situation, and there were a lot of things that she said that broke my heart, but the thing that stood out the most was when she confessed, "I just don't feel like I have a purpose in this world. I just feel like my existence is meaningless."

If you are a person who feels that way, you have meaning as a believer in that God allowed you to contain his faith. He placed it inside of you. What a thought, that God would use earthen vessels to contain his faith. How fortunate we are. Are you aware that Christianity is the only prevalent faith that speaks of the body and not just the spirit as a tool of God? I don't know why God would use this flesh that is so much a part of this world. I can't understand that.

We are made out of this world. The carbon and the molecules and the other elements that make up your body are the same things that make up that tree standing outside. Isn't that encouraging? You are a part of this world. In fact, according to modern day scientists, if you took the average adult male and broke him down into his component chemicals and substances, those chemicals and substances could be bought for no more than two dollars and fifty cents. According to one professor at a major university, our human bodies are a part of this universe and they are not really very significant. In the vastness of the universe, they are simply a wave, a wiggle, a localized disturbance that is just a part of everything else.

Do you have meaning? Yes you have meaning. What is the meaning of your life? God looked down on you--a wave, a wiggle, nothing more than some water and chemical--and placed the faith of his Son inside of you, and when that happened you became an important soldier for Jesus Christ. Now it's time to start serving.

WE ARE CALLED TO THE FAITH

Jude is talking to those who are called. I think we are all glad that we've been called because it means that one day we can go to heaven, but not too many of us are glad we've been called to service. We don't want to work.

Let's just be honest for a moment. Do you really know what it's like to be called by God? Haven't you ever heard the telephone ring and when you answered it, you suddenly wished you hadn't? There have been times in my life when my plans for the whole day have been ruined because I simply picked up the phone when I could have let it ring.

When you answer God's call to service, sometimes it will destroy your plans, and you'll wish that you had never answered the phone; but at the end of the day, answering God's call always turns out to have been a good thing. It's better his way.

The only reason you and I are saved is because all throughout history men and women of God have been earnestly contending for the faith. David didn't walk off the battlefield at the sight of a nine-foot Goliath because he knew that on that battlefield he was earnestly contending for the faith. Shedrach, Meshack and Abednego had no problem walking steadily into a fiery furnace, because in that furnace they were earnestly contending for the faith. Jeremiah kept on serving the Lord even when he went for years without a single response, because he was earnestly contending for the faith. Daniel had no trouble spending the night in a lions' den because in that den he was earnestly contending for the faith. Jesus Christ died for the sins of the world because on that cross he was earnestly contending for the faith. The disciples all, save one, died a martyr's death, because in their final moments they were earnestly contending for the faith that had been entrusted to them.

He's calling you today. Some of you he is calling to service. He wants you to do something for him to contend for the faith. It's your job. You've been entrusted with it. He is calling you. Will you continue to let the phone ring or will you answer him today?

The reason that this section of the book is devoted to the discussion of false doctrines is because of this very thing. It has been demonstrated that there is a God and that he is Jesus. Now we must defend the true faith by discussing which version of Jesus is the true one. Each of the false doctrines selected are representative of a certain false belief about Jesus and must be confronted. The choices of particular faiths such as Mormonism, are not capricious but rather were made because the named faith represents one or several misunderstood philosophies which are true of many false doctrines. As we study this section, please keep in mind that Jude warned about these false ideas centuries ago. Light exposes what is in the shadows. In this section, it is clear that the blinding light of scripture exposes the truth of these false beliefs.

Chapter 11: Jehovah's Witnesses

It would be an unlikely task to examine every false doctrine that exists regarding the personality of Jesus Christ. Thus, it is needful to consider those arguments that represent the major false theological teachings held by others and then debunk them according to logic and special scriptural revelation. Until this point, we have been prohibited from using special revelation (scripture) for determining truth. Moving now to discuss invalid reports about who Jesus was and or is, we are able to appeal to special revelation because the Bible is held by many of these faiths to be the Word of God in some legitimate form. Furthermore, having determined that there is a God and that Jesus is divine beyond a reasonable doubt, logic permits us to now hold the Bible in high esteem.

A disclaimer should be presented at this point. I realize that a critique of other pseudo-Christian beliefs is not popular in our day. I also realize that there is much controversy among religious people about whether or not such doctrines should be challenged. It would seem that harmony among religions is considered a precious jewel in our modern society. However, let it be stated clearly, that absolute truth should not be sacrificed merely to protect the feelings of others. If heaven and hell are indeed in question, then these truths must be discussed. After all, we owe it to our religious heritage to protect the true faith which has been handed down to us.

The first persecution of the church came in AD 67 when Nero would take Christians and sew them in the skins of wild animals and let dogs gnaw at them until they expired. He then placed them in shirts dipped in wax so that they were stiff and then fixed them to trees, lighting them on fire to illuminate his gardens at night.

We owe our spiritual ancestors our efforts.

In AD 249, the common method of killing Christians was to sew them up in a burlap style bag full of serpents and scorpions and cast the person into the sea.

We owe our spiritual ancestors our best efforts.

Perhaps you've heard the story of Agatha, an early Christian, who refused to give herself sexually to the emperor because of her religious virtues and was therefore torn apart with hooks, singed deep with hot pokers and laid on live coals intermingled with glass until she died.

These are grizzly details about a sad time, but they are factual. History reveals that believers in times past were so committed to what they held that no price was too great. In part, their suffering occurred so that a pristine faith could be delivered to you and me in absolute truth. Ungratefully, many believers today would ignore the relevance of the same truths for which others have died. For this reason, in the next few chapters we will discuss some of the major challenges that have been made about who Christ was (is), and for this task we shall, at times, examine specific faiths which represent such untruths.

Who are the Jehovah's Witnesses? If we are to discuss false teachings about Jesus, a phrase must be remembered, "If you're wrong about Jesus, it doesn't matter what you're right about." Because we have shown that Jesus is divinely the centerpiece of all creation, what is said about him must be absolutely and perfectly preserved truth. No pseudo-Christian faith has more distorted the person of Jesus than those who refer to themselves as Jehovah's Witnesses. Many of the truths they hold are accurate and acceptable to mainstream Christianity. Their passion for personal evangelism, regular assembly, apologetic arguments and supernatural experience are to be admired. Yet, in the midst of their zeal, they have forfeited the most precious and logical being in all of history, namely the man Christ Jesus.

THEIR NAME

And when he had found him, he brought him unto Antioch. And it came to pass, that the whole year they assembled themselves with the church, and taught much people. And the disciples were called Christians first at Antioch." (Acts 11:26)

It was during the year of 1931 that they adopted the name, "Jehovah's Witnesses." However, there is no such being on earth as a Jehovah Witness. Witness comes from the Latin word, "testor," which means, "I testify," and Jesus said, "***We speak that we do know, and testify that we have seen" (John 3:11)*** Thus, we see from the plain statement of Jesus himself that we *testify* about things that we have personally observed with human eyes. Therefore, according to Jesus, one will have had to see Jehovah in order to become a Jehovah Witness.

Now consider this, there is no single account of anyone having ever seen Jehovah God with human or spiritual eyes in any biblical or extra biblical history. Knee-jerk reactions are common when this statement is made. We are so accustomed to hearing God spoken about in human terms that we mistakenly consider him to look like a man. Not so! God the Father is not made of flesh and blood and has no discernable body at all. This is true for a variety of reasons, both observable in general (nature) and special (scripture) revelation.

In the first section, we discussed the law of causality and determined that the universe exists of time, space and matter. Because of this, the cause of the universe must be something not constrained by time, not existing in space and *not made of matter!* The result is that the Creator of the universe must be what the religious community would refer to as spiritual. In simpler terms, if God created material things, He cannot be material because he existed prior to materiality.

Moreover, scripture attests to the spirituality (non-materiality) of God:

"God is a Spirit: and they that worship him must worship him in spirit and in truth." John 4:24

You might argue, "I heard a preacher on TV say that Moses saw Jehovah God or that Elijah saw Jehovah or Adam saw Jehovah." Keep in mind the question is not, "Has anybody ever seen God?" The question is, "Has anybody ever seen Jehovah (God the Father)?" What's the difference? Jesus is the portion of the Godhead (trinity) that represents the material personification of God. Thus, when God is seen in a human form in the Old Testament, this (theophany) is Jesus. But no one has ever seen Jehovah God with human eyes for he is a spiritual being. Hence, there is no such thing as a Jehovah Witness.

You say, "Well then, what are they?" If you are a "Jehovah Witness," then you were originally called a "Russellite" because the founder of your group's name was Charles Taze Russell. But true believers in the One True God have a name. According to Acts 11:26, we are Christians.

If God were to appear before you today and shine a holy light on you, would he see written across your forehead the name, Christian, an evident sign that this one belongs to Christ. Or would he find nothing. You say, "Oh no, no, no. I'M A CHRISTIAN! That much I'm sure of." That may be true for many believers reading this book, but sadly, if I were to shine that holy light on you, I might find "Christian" but where it once was plainly visible, it has now been covered up and caked over and faded. That is to say, you may be a Christian but nobody would know it examining your life.

I went to the national convention of a large Christian denomination recently, and there I heard a man preach who was raised the son of a Muslim Holy man. He knew the Qu'ran back and forth. He knew about Jesus. And, as far as he was concerned,

Jesus was nothing more than a prophet. This man came to America as a missionary to us for their faith. He was unshakeable in what he believed and could not be turned. Do you know what finally won him to Christ? It was one high school kid who loved the Lord and would not shut up about it. He said that the kid loved him to Christ.

If you bear the name of Christ, you are Jesus' representative. You are not a Hunterite, a Bushite, a Kerryite, an Oprahite or a Russellite. You are a Christian. Do you wear the name proudly?

Their Kingdom

"But into whatsoever city ye enter, and they receive you not, go your ways out into the streets of the same, and say,

Even the very dust of your city, which cleaveth on us, we do wipe off against you: notwithstanding be ye sure of this, that the kingdom of God is come nigh unto you." Luke 10:10, 11

Not only do we have a different name, but we've also got a different kingdom. See, here lies the difference. The Jehovah Witness says that Jesus has no kingdom on earth. When Christ comes back, according the Jehovah Witnesses, only then will he have a kingdom. Aside from the simple fact that if he's king he's got to be king of something, and if he's really got no kingdom, then we're fools to call him king, we must find out if we are a part of a kingdom or not.

Let us turn to the pages of inspiration and see what God has to say about these things. First, does Christ have a kingdom now? Well, about two thousand years ago, John the Baptist preached until his death concerning the time when the kingdom would come:

"In those days came John the Baptist, preaching in the wilderness of Judea

And saying, Repent ye: for the kingdom of heaven is at hand." (Matt. 3:1, 2) John preached the kingdom was *at hand.* Did he preach the truth? God sent John, therefore John's message came from God, but did he preach the truth?

The truth is that the kingdom is already here.

In traveling to modern day Israel, it can be discovered that there is no king among the Jewish community. Strangely, there should be. But there has not been a king in thousands of years. After the Jews returned to Jerusalem and began to establish it following the last captivity mentioned in the Old Testament, some interesting things took place. The intertestamental period is how biblical historians describe the time period between the end of the Old Testament and the beginning of the new. However, much happened in Israel during this time.

Importantly, Antiochus Epiphany, an evil ruler, overtook the Holy City and defiled the temple. In an act of absolute blasphemy, he sacrificed a sow on the altar of God, utterly destroying the morale of the Israelites. For a time, the Jews were beaten until one godly priest refused to bend a knee to Antiochus. A messenger was sent to this priest urging him to pledge allegiance to the new ruler of Jerusalem, but when the messenger arrived, the priest of God killed him and proceeded to pull down the pagan idols. The priest's son is a famous historical figure among the Jews even until this day, and his name was Judas Maccabbees, "the hammer." Assuming his father's mantle, he secretly trained an army of Israelites and led a revolt into the Holy City which ended with the assassination of Antiochus and the cleansing of the temple. After the massacre had ended, lamp stands were placed all over the temple and the legend holds that they miraculously burned for eight days without being refilled. For this reason, today the Jewish symbol, called the menorah, is commonplace and the festival of lights (Hannukah) is observed annually. Israel has now reinstated every attribute they had once held except the rule of a king.

The king they should have instated would have been a Hebrew boy in the direct line of King David. Strangely, this final piece of the Jewish puzzle was not enacted. The Roman governing over Jerusalem confounded this problem considerably. So, who should have been the king of the Jews? More accurately, who was the child in the direct line of King David? The answer is found in God's Word.

The book of the generation of Jesus Christ, the son of David, the son of Abraham.

Abraham begat Isaac; and Isaac begat Jacob; and Jacob begat Judas and his brethren;

And Judas begat Phares and Zara of Thamar; and Phares begat Esrom; and Esrom begat Aram;

And Aram begat Aminadab; and Aminadab begat Naasson; and Naasson begat Salmon;

And Salmon begat Booz of Rachab; and Booz begat Obed of Ruth; and Obed begat Jesse;

And Jesse begat David the king; and David the king begat Solomon of her that had been the wife of Urias;

And Solomon begat Roboam; and Roboam begat Abia; and Abia begat Asa;

And Asa begat Josaphat; and Josaphat begat Joram; and Joram begat Ozias;

And Ozias begat Joatham; and Joatham begat Achaz; and Achaz begat Ezekias;

And Ezekias begat Manasses; and Manasses begat Amon; and Amon begat Josias;

And Josias begat Jechonias and his brethren, about the time they were carried away to Babylon:

And after they were brought to Babylon, Jechonias begat Salathiel; and Salathiel begat Zorobabel;

And Zorobabel begat Abiud; and Abiud begat Eliakim; and Eliakim begat Azor;

And Azor begat Sadoc; and Sadoc begat Achim; and Achim begat Eliud;

And Eliud begat Eleazar; and Eleazar begat Matthan; and Matthan begat Jacob;

And Jacob begat Joseph the husband of Mary, of whom was born Jesus, who is called Christ.

So all the generations from Abraham to David are fourteen generations; and from David until the carrying away into

Babylon are fourteen generations; and from the carrying away into Babylon unto Christ are fourteen generations.

– Matt.1:1-17

Jewish scholars will seldom argue with this historical genealogy of the line of David. Joseph, an impoverished carpenter from Bethlehem, should have been the king of the Jews during his day, yet because of the political situation described above, he was overlooked. His first child (by birth *or adoption*) according to Hebrew law, should have been the rightful heir to his throne. Moreover, Mary was also in the direct line of King David. Resulting from this, we have two separate genealogies which should have led to Christ's kingship. Fulfilling prophecies mentioned in previous chapters, the Romans placed a sign over the head of Christ declaring his kingship at the crucifixion. So why do the Jews not have a king today? The answer is simple; they do have a king. A new king is only instituted when the existing king has died, and what most Israelis will not recognize is that the previous king (Jesus) is not dead but lives and will live forever. Clearly, Jesus has an earthly and a spiritual kingdom as indicated by scripture, logic and politics, yet the Russellite faith claims that Jesus' kingdom has not yet been instituted. Even without aspiring to the first religious or spiritual argument, this is just factually wrong.

Can I be honest with you? I have had certain people in churches that I have pastored become angry with me for confronting such false ideologies as those just discussed. However, if Jesus is not Lord, as held by the Russellites, but rather one of many prophets, then there is no reason to believe that we can be saved by faith through Jesus. Yet, that is what scripture claims.

If ye shall confess with your mouth that Jesus is Lord and believe in thine heart that God hath raised Him from the dead ye shall be saved. Romans 10:9.

As controversial and unpopular as it is to confront these truths, it is beneficial and necessary to do so if we are to preserve the faith that has been delivered to us from our religious ancestors. Moreover, we have been warned of false teachers who would distort the divine nature of Jesus.

For there are certain men crept in unawares, who were before of old ordained to this condemnation, ungodly men, turning the grace of our God into lasciviousness, and denying the only Lord God, and our Lord Jesus Christ. – Jude 1:4

The truth must be proclaimed even if it is labeled intolerant, unkind, hateful or controversial.

I want to make a confession to you that might make it a little clearer why I am concerned with false doctrine the way I am. It might surprise you to know that I had a drug problem when I was a teenager. That's right. My parents drug me to church and drug me to Sunday School and drug me to youth camp. Thank God for parents like that.

Not everyone was so fortunate. I've got a friend from high school with whom I shared some of the most wonderful moments of my life, and now because of our culture's tolerance for unbiblical teachings in other churches, he's accepted a life of homosexuality. I know people who, because some other church messed with their brain, have now committed suicide.

We enjoy religious freedom in America, and because of this, I have been told that I am unpatriotic for speaking out against other faiths. No sir, I'll fight for your right to put whatever kind of crazy church or mosque wherever you desire. That is patriotism, but forcing me to agree with it or remain silent about it is religious slavery.

This is a jihad, a holy war. And we're in it.

Let me say it this way, we, as Christians, have become too nice. We're so nice that we are more concerned with an Iraqi having underwear pulled over his head by U.S. soldiers than we are with Nick Burg's head being slowly severed from his shoulders. The difference is that our people acted against their commander and chief, they acted against the Geneva Convention, and they are being court-martialed for it, while the men who severed Nick Burg's head are hailed as heroes.

"Well," you might say, "I don't want all of that in our church. Why can't we just have a nice mild-mannered sermon by a nice mild-mannered preacher about how we can all be more mild-mannered?" That sounds like someone without a kingdom to me. Jesus says we've got a kingdom, and a kingdom must have an army.

I want to be clear about my position. There is a difference between bearing spiritual fruit and being a religious nut. I do not believe that any violence should be done to those who believe in false doctrine. The jihad that I am referring to is a spiritual battle and scripture promotes it:

> ***For we wrestle not against flesh and blood, but against principalities, against powers, against the rulers of the darkness of this world, against spiritual wickedness in high places. – Ephesians 6:12***

This is a war. Lives, livelihoods and people's souls are at stake. Are you fighting for the kingdom?

THEIR PARADISE

"And I heard the number of them which were sealed: and there were sealed an hundred and forty and four thousand of all the tribes of the children of Israel"

"After this I beheld, and, lo, a great multitude, which no man could number, of all nations, and kindreds, and people, and tongues, stood before the throne, and before the Lamb, clothed with white robes, and palms in their hands;" **(Revelation 7:4,9)**

According to the Russellite Faith, in 1914 all of those who were Jehovah Witnesses were supposed to be caught up and 144,000 taken to heaven. After that initial 144,000, everyone that was saved would live here on earth, and the earth would be restored to the condition it was in when Adam was in the Garden of Eden.

Clearly, that did not happen and the prophecy was false. The 144,000 represents only the number of Jews that will be sealed (saved) in the end times. Thus, according to the Russellites, you're not going to heaven; you're going to live right here on earth. But I have learned something throughout my human existence that is true of all men. I've got needs that no food can fulfill, that no fluid can fulfill, that no thrill can fulfill and that no medicine can fulfill. Something must meet that need and it is not of this world. I like what C.S. Lewis said in his book, Mere Christianity:

> "If I find in myself a desire which no experience in this world can satisfy, the most probable explanation is that I was made for another world."[1]

However, the truth is that some people would rather have it the way they have it right now on planet earth. They'd rather stay here than ascend to paradise. You might say, "Well, that's right. Why would I ever want to go there?"

In one of his books, A.M. Hunter, the New Testament scholar, relates the story of a dying man who asked his Christian doctor to tell him something about the place to which he was going. As the doctor fumbled for a reply, he heard a scratching at the door, and he had his answer. "Do you hear that?" he asked his patient. "It's my dog. I left him downstairs, but he has grown impatient, and has come up and hears my voice. He has no notion what is inside this door, but he knows that I am here. Isn't it the same with you? You don't know what lies beyond the door, but you know that your Master is there."[2]

I want to go to heaven for one reason. Jesus will be there.

Their Punishment

Finally, according to the Russellites there will be no everlasting punishment for those who do not accept Christ but, rather, they will merely be destroyed.

***"Then shall he say also unto them on the left hand, depart from me, ye cursed, into everlasting fire, prepared for the devil and his angels:"* (Matthew 25:41)**

Special revelation (scripture) indicates that there will be eternal separation from God for those who do not trust him. As unpopular as the idea of hell may be to some people today, it is a reality if we are to trust special revelation, which is trustworthy for reasons mentioned previously in this section.

Summary

From debunking the Russellite faith, several things can be concluded about Jesus. First, he is the physical manifestation of God appearing both in the Old and New Testaments. Second, he is God operating in the human experience and at no point less than Jehovah. Third, Christ has a kingdom which is already established in the world as evident by special revelation, good logic and politics. Fourth, the acceptance of Christ's divinity is paramount to salvation. Fifth, living outside of Christ's eternal kingdom (heaven) is an option for man, but the only alternative is hell (simply defined for now as the absence of God.) For these reasons, I demand that the blinding lights expose the falsehoods of this system of beliefs.

[1]Lewis, C.S. ***Mere Christianity***. Macmillan press.

[2]Hunter, A.M. ***Introducing the New Testament***. SCM press Ltd.

Chapter 12: Mormonism

"Jesus saith unto him, I am the way, the truth, and the life: no man cometh unto the Father, but by me. If ye had known me, ye should have known my father also: and from henceforth ye known him, and have seen him

Philip sayeth unto him, Lord, shew us the father, and it sufficeth us.

Jesus saith unto him, have I been so long time with you, and yet, hast thou not known me, Philip? He that hath seen me hath seen the father; and how sayest thou then, Shew us the Father?" (John 14:6-9)

I wonder how many of us could say that we have never made a mistake.

I remember one girl I dated as a teenager. We were riding bicycles and she thought it would be cute for me to ride with her sitting atop the handlebars like people do sometimes. After we failed our attempts to make that work twice, I said, "You know, I just don't think I can do that with someone who weighs more than me."

People make mistakes.

A few years ago a lady named Michelle in a church I was pastoring called the church office, and when I answered the phone she said, "Hello Brother Braxton, this is your problem church member."

And I immediately said, "This must be Michelle."

People make mistakes

When my mother was trying to recover from hip surgery, we were in her room watching the evening news together. I thought, "What could I say that would make my mother feel better?"

She said, "You know, usually those news ladies are so beautiful."

I thought, "That's it." I was about to say, "Mom, you could be one of those ladies because you're as beautiful as they are."

But before I could get it out, she said, "But tonight these ladies look tired and worn down."

And I chimed in and said, "Yeah, you could even be one of them."

People make mistakes. We all make mistakes, but if we're going to make mistakes, let us make our mistakes over the dinner table. Let us make our mistakes on the golf course. Let us make our mistakes at the supermarket, but for heaven's sake, make no mistake about Jesus Christ the Son of the living God.

In this chapter, we are talking in part about the Mormon church and what they are. But more importantly, above any sectarian faith or denomination we seek to discuss, what can be seen in special revelation about Jesus Christ is vital.

Orthodox Christians have believed for centuries that Jesus Christ is no less than God. He is co-eternal with God and shares his primary attributes. Yet, at a point in time, he laid aside certain attributes of his omnipotence and made himself a man, being conceived by the Holy Spirit supernaturally in the womb of the virgin, Mary. However, this is not what is held by the Mormon church.

I was directed by the Mormon church on Underwood Rd. in McMinnville, Tennessee, to their website which explains: "By contrast, **the Mormon Church teaches that Jesus Christ is our elder brother who progressed to godhood, having first been procreated as a spirit child by a Heavenly Father and a heavenly mother; He was later conceived physically through intercourse between the Heavenly Father and the virgin Mary**" (Achieving a Celestial Marriage, p. 129; Mormon Doctrine, pp. 546-547; 742). Mormon doctrine affirms that Jesus and Lucifer are brothers

(Gospel Principles, pp. 17-18; Mormon Doctrine, p. 192).

If what the Mormon church teaches is true, then we must forfeit what we believe as Christians and join their congregation. However, if mainstream Christianity is correct and Christ did not just become God, but was always God through the trinity, then this false teaching must be exposed.

The Philosophical Argument Against Mormonism

According to Mormon teaching, there is a plurality of gods. That is to say, anyone can become a god that is co-equal with God the father. Mormonism, then, is a polytheistic religion. Polytheism in every case is false for the following reasons. It will be demonstrated below why scripture does not promote the idea that there are many gods; however, it should also be noted that good logic also prohibits this idea. Philosophically we can know that there may only be one God because of the very meaning of the terms stated. The word, "God," universally refers to a supreme being. Some philosophers have defined God as the being of which none greater can be thought. If this is a universally accepted fact, we must understand that if there were more than one, one could not be more powerful or less complete than any other God. This is a logical impossibility. If gods are different, as polytheism always holds, then by virtue of their differences, each god would lack something that other gods possessed, otherwise there would be no differences and they would be exactly the same. Resulting from this is the clear understanding that there may only be one truly Supreme Being.

The Testimony Of The Gospel

Now the birth of Jesus Christ was on this wise: When as his mother Mary was espoused to Joseph, before they came together, she was found with child of the Holy Ghost.

Then Joseph her husband, being a just man, and not willing to make her a public example, was minded to put her away privily.

But while he thought on these things, behold, the angel of the LORD appeared unto him in a dream, saying, Joseph, thou son of David, fear not to take unto thee Mary thy wife: for that which is conceived in her is of the Holy Ghost.

> *And she shall bring forth a son, and thou shalt call his name JESUS: for he shall save his people from their sins.*
>
> *Now all this was done, that it might be fulfilled which was spoken of the Lord by the prophet, saying,*
>
> *Behold, a virgin shall be with child, and shall bring forth a son, and they shall call his name Emmanuel, which being interpreted is, God with us.*
>
> **(Matthew 1:18-23)**

I want to remind you of the key idea of this entire section. It is summed up in this phrase, "If you're wrong about Jesus it doesn't matter what you are right about." Either Jesus is the virgin-born Son of God conceived by the Holy Spirit and has always been divine, or he is something else.

You might say, "What real difference does it make how Jesus came to be? Is it really all that important about these minor beliefs?" According to Jesus it was.

Two men, Robert and James, applied for an engineering position. Both applicants having the same qualifications were asked to take a test by the department manager. Upon completion of the exam both men only missed one of the questions. The manager went to Robert and said, "Thank you for your interest, but we've decided to give James the job." Robert replied, "Why? We both correctly answered nine questions. I believe I should get this job, especially since I've grown up in this town and James just moved here." The manager said, "We made our decision not on the correct answers, but on the question you missed." "How could one incorrect answer be better than the other?," asked Robert. "Simple," said the manager. "James put down on question #5, 'I don't know', and you put down, 'Neither do I.'"

We can't possibly have more than one way of true faith. As with Robert and James, logic indicates that when two opposing views are in sight, one or both must be wrong. Someone is a deceiver and the truth must be exposed.

Most people believe that the Mormon congregation has only one holy book, that being the Bible. Some who are more knowledgeable about Mormonism are aware of the Book of Mormon as well. Actually the Mormons have four sacred texts on which they place their faith. The scriptures they cling to are known as (1) the Bible (2) the Book of Mormon (3) Doctrines and Covenants (D&C) and (4) Pearls of Great price (PGP). Though the Book of Mormon receives the most attention the (D&C) and (PGP) are considered to be God-inspired as well. What is surprising to most is that almost all of these supposed sacred writings have been discredited.

First, it should be mentioned that the claims of the writings are ridiculous no matter what religious background you have. According to the book of Mormon in 800 B.C. a group of Hebrews boarded a great ship and set sail toward a new promised land that God would reveal. They sailed south and across the Indian and pacific oceans and landed in Central America. This is the origin of the Mayans, Aztecs and Native Americans. These travelers populated the region and then fought each other in a great war which ended with the written record of all that occurred being buried in a hill in New York state inscribed on golden plates. Thousands of years later Joseph Smith would be led to that site by an angel and retrieve the plates which contained the book of Mormon. Among other things, the book demands that the new promised land complete with a great temple should be in Independence, Missouri.

The Primary problem with the Book of Mormon is that it gives no way of verifying its authenticity, as does the Bible. Furthermore, its claims are so outlandish that no logical person would ever take them on faith simply because eleven men claimed to have seen them. The (PGP) is simply a collection of wisdom writing from Joseph Smith and amended by several other (prophets). The (D&C) was written as a result of a purchase made by Joseph Smith while in Cincinnati, Ohio. There he encountered a Native American trader who had in his possession a scroll that was indeed from ancient Egypt. Joseph Smith with the help of God translated this scroll and demanded that it contained the writings of Abraham about the coming Mormon church. Unfortunately for Smith, the study of Egyptian hieroglyphics had not yet been mastered. When it was Egyptologists discovered that the one page scroll simply had to do with how a certain burial style in Egypt was to be handled. Clearly this discredited the entire (D&C). These four documents are known as the Quad and the only one that is historically verifiable is the Bible.

According to the book of Mormon in 1 Nephi, the Bible is missing many of its important parts, but what is contained is inspired truth. This means that even though it is the assertion of the Mormon faith that the traditional protestant Bible is incomplete, they claim to believe that it is, in part, the Word of God. So, we must ask the question, " Does what they believe measure up to the scripture?"

My father was at Brigham Young's home which is now a museum. Brigham Young was the man who started the university that bears his name. It is a Mormon institution. When touring the house, a very distinguished Mormon man said to him, "Sir, I know that you are a Baptist preacher and I have studied your faith and am comfortable with mine, but what would you say is fundamentally the difference between your belief and that of the Mormons?"

My father said, "Well, we don't have time to get into all the theological implications but basically there is one difference."

"What is that?" the man said.

To which my father responded, "I'm going to heaven and you're going to hell."

Now, granted this was a harsh statement, but one made tongue in cheek. Both men had a laugh. Still, it demonstrates the severity of the question posed above. Does the Mormon church have a scriptural faith? What does The Bible say?

> *I have glorified thee on the earth: I have finished the work which thou gavest me to do.*
>
> *And now, O Father, glorify thou me with thine own self with the glory which I had with thee before the world was.* **(John 17:4,5)**
>
> *Beware lest any man spoil you through philosophy and vain deceit, after the tradition of men, after the rudiments of the world, and not after Christ.*
>
> *For in him dwelleth all the fulness of the Godhead bodily.*
>
> *(Colossians 2:8,9)*

Friend, I cannot hide from it and I cannot avoid it. I cannot keep silent of it-- the testimony of the gospel is that Jesus Christ is and always has been God himself. If you're wrong about Jesus, it doesn't matter what you're right about.

If what the Bible says is true, then you must be worshipping Jesus Christ as God, or without him there is no hope for you! I was touched because just recently I had a child say to me, "How do I know if I am saved." Reader, if when you commit sin, there is not something inside of you that calls out, "This is wrong; this is not right. I've got to get rid of this sin and get right with Jesus," then it is an indication that you have not the Spirit of God and thus are lost and outside of his eternal kingdom.

The testimony of the Gospel is that Christ is and always was God.

The Testimony Of Christ

"*I and my Father are one.*" (John 10:30)

Jesus makes the claim again and again that he is God, that he and God are one being together and that there is none else. In the Old Testament, God made the first commandment, "You shall have no other gods before me." The message of the scripture is that there is one God and Jesus is that God. However, according to the Mormon Church:

There are many Gods (Book of Abraham 4:3ff), **and that we can become gods and goddesses in**

the celestial kingdom (*Doctrine and Covenants* 132:19-20; *Gospel Principles*, p. 245; *Achieving a Celestial Marriage*, p. 130). It also teaches that **those who achieve godhood will have spirit children who will worship and pray to them, just as we worship and pray to God the Father** (Gospel Principles, p. 302).

I like what one seminary professor once said. He had been teaching about the danger of blaspheming God's Son by claiming that he is anything less than God. He told how for some the earth opened, for some fire fell from heaven, and for some floods came. He told the class that he had one response when false cults came to proclaim their heresy: "I have just paid off my house and enjoy it very much. If you are going to continue to spout evil doctrine that will anger the God of the universe, at least get off of my porch!"

Even the Mormon church claims that we can trust the words of Jesus Christ. And if that is so, then we must understand that what Christ has said in this verse is true. There is only one God and he is presented in the form of Jesus Christ. I want you to notice the singularity of the word "the" in this verse:

"I am the way, I am the Truth, I am the light and no man cometh unto the father but by Me." (John 14:6)

Neither is there salvation in any other: for there is none other name under heaven given among men, whereby we must be saved." **(Acts 4:12)**

The Angels around the throne of God chant, "***Holy Holy Holy is the Lord God almighty who was and is and is to come***" (Rev. 4:8), and if that's true of him and he always was then he didn't become God. We can trust in God the Father and Jesus Christ as the means of reaching him.

Some of you might say, "Well, I'd never believe something like Mormonism." Perhaps you wouldn't, but there are many people who have seen the truth of salvation, have seen that they need Jesus, have denied him again and again and have no intention of trusting in him despite where the evidence may lead. Hear this, friend. Whatever you are believing in outside of Christ has already been demonstrated as illogical and futile, thus it is just as silly as the belief posited by Mormonism. Without Christ's presence in the life of a man, that man is destined for separation from God.

When a baby's diaper needs to be changed, what does that baby do to notify his parent? He cries. What is another way that one can know that a baby needs to be changed? When a baby needs to be changed, not only does that baby know that it needs to be changed, but so does everyone else that is within smelling range of that baby.

Isn't it interesting, though, how sometimes when people need to be changed, everyone else around knows it except for the person that needs the changing? Why is that? When that baby starts to cry, it is because something deep down inside-- somewhere-- just doesn't feel right. Something just isn't sitting the way it's supposed to sit. He doesn't know what it is but something's wrong, and so that baby cries out to its mother and in his own little way says, "I need to be changed. Please change me."

In that same way, if a man truly has Jesus working in his life, but allows himself to go on day after day not growing in his Christianity, and not always being changed by that fire that God has placed in his life, there will be something inside of him that says, "Hey, this just doesn't feel right. This isn't how it's supposed to be. I don't know what's wrong, but I need to be changed. Jesus, change me!" If that does not happen, it means that there is no Holy Spirit at home in that man's life and if he died, he would not spend eternity with God.

By the testimony of the Gospel, without the understanding that Jesus is the one true God, there is no hope for a successful eternity. By the testimony of Christ himself and without such an acceptance of that truth, there is no hope. I'm asking you today, the most important question you'll ever be asked, "Are you absolutely sure that you have him?"

The Testimony of God

"While he yet spake, behold, a bright cloud overshadowed them: and behold a voice out of the cloud, which said, This is my beloved Son, in whom I am well pleased; hear ye him".
(Matt. 17:5)

We are all children of God once we are saved, but Christ is the unique form of God on earth. If we were to become gods, as the Mormons say, then when we were saved, we would all hear a voice from heaven speaking to us in this way.

According to the McMinnville Mormon Church website, "Before you were born, you lived with your Heavenly Father as one of his beloved spirit children. You knew and loved him."

The truth of scripture is that he formed you in the womb.

Thus saith the LORD, thy redeemer, and he that formed thee from the womb, I am the LORD that maketh all things; that stretcheth forth the heavens alone; that spreadeth abroad the earth by myself; - Isaiah 44:24

> **Before I formed thee in the belly I knew thee; and before thou camest forth out of the womb I sanctified thee, and I ordained thee a prophet unto the nations. – Jeremiah 1:5**

Sadly, the great mistake of the Mormons is that they have discovered pieces of the truth but ignored that truth for something created by man.

> "Men occasionally stumble over the truth, but most of them pick themselves up and hurry off as if nothing happened." - Winston Churchill

Each week, as a pastor, I saw people walk out of the church building and into eternity—some I never saw again and some I saw week after week refusing to make the decision that God was calling them to make. They tripped over pieces of the truth and then scurried off. Don't be wrong about Jesus.

John Newton was a rough, dirty sailor with a foul mouth and an appetite for rotten living. He hated life and life hated him. He was captain of a slave ship. Then someone placed in his hands a copy of Thomas a Kempis,' The Imitation of Christ. He also had the gift of a good mother who told him about the Savior when he was young. And then he was saved. He went all over England sharing his faith. Well past his "retirement" age, he had to have an assistant stand in the pulpit with him on Sundays. He was nearly blind and spoke in whispers, but nothing could keep him from preaching while he still had breath.

One Sunday, while delivering his message, he repeated the sentence: "Jesus Christ is precious." His helper whispered to him: "But you have already said that twice." Newton turned to his helper and said loudly, "Yes, I've said it twice, and I'm going to say it again." The stones in the ancient sanctuary fairly shook as the grand old preacher said again: "Jesus Christ is precious!"[4]

[1]Smith, Joseph. ***The Book of Mormon: Another Testament of Jesus Christ***. The

Church of Jesus Christ of Latter-Day Saints.

[2]***Doctrines and Covenants.*** Herald Publishing House.

[3]Smith, Joseph. ***Pears of Great Price***. Filiquarian Publishing.

[4]Source Unknown

Chapter 13: Salvation By Works

At this point it is profitable for us to consider the needfulness of man to trust Christ alone in order to receive salvation from his fallen position. Never ending is the list of pseudo-Christian faiths that attempt to add some human endeavor to the work of Christ in the saving process. Accept the challenge to investigate the number of people in your own life who claim to be believers, and you will likely discover that eighty percent of them or more believe that there is more to salvation than a simple trust in Christ. Conversely, the hyper-Calvinist, to be discussed later, argues that there is nothing done on the part of man, not even belief, that will help to appropriate salvation. These sorts of extreme "all or nothing" views are not only biblically inaccurate but also logically implausible.

Proper soteriology leads us to the understanding that no human work is involved in the redemptive process. Neither prayer, church membership, knowledge of scripture, moral deeds, ethical living, eucharistic endeavors nor baptism will result in the salvation of a man for reasons to be discussed in this chapter. However, contrary to the view of the extreme Calvinist, one thing must be true of the person hoping to identify with Christ. That one thing is trust.

Now I realize that even those who have, until now, agreed with most of what has been said, may not like this statement of trust. Even in the churches that are most biblical in their theological persuasion and doctrine, there is a belief that some sort of prayer must be prayed. Indeed it is my practice to encourage men and women to verbally repent of sin; however, scripture teaches that the salvation occurs when man simply trusts Christ. What is belief?

> **"He that believeth and is baptized shall be saved; but he that believeth not shall be damned". - Mark 16:16**

You will notice the seeming indication that one must be baptized in order to be saved. We will discuss the implications of this passage regarding baptism later in the chapter. For now, notice the word " believeth." It is the Greek word, "pisteuo," which is the same word used in the New Testament for "trust." Strangely, we have made much of the differences between the two words, "believe" and "trust" in our modern day when in truth there was no difference to the original hearer. Thus, what is required for salvation is simply trusting that Christ is the way and that he will save you. The problem that the extreme or hyper-Calvinist would have is that this too is considered a work of man. Yet, trust alone is not a work. It is a mental process requiring no effort on the part of an individual but rather a willingness to accept what will be done by another.

Romans 10:9 is the last hurdle over which we must bound if we are to accept the premise that no human work, including prayer, is required.

"That if thou shalt confess with thy mouth the Lord Jesus, and shalt believe in thine heart that God hath raised him from the dead, thou shalt be saved." – Romans 10:9

Let me start by demanding that this passage does have implications for the salvation process. Proper exegesis demands that we understand to whom this passage was written if we are to gather what it could mean for us today. Romans chapters nine through eleven are clearly written to a specific group. That group was the people of Israel.

> *"Brethren, my heart's desire and prayer to God for Israel is, that they might be saved."*
> *– Romans 10:1*

Understanding this is paramount to so much that is contained therein. While it is commonly held that the word, "saved," mentioned in this passage can and should be applied to Christ's redemptive work at Calvary, it must also be noted that this was probably as much a reference to national salvation from earthly harm. Note the distinction made in verse eleven:

> *"For with the heart man believeth unto righteousness; and with the mouth confession is made unto salvation". - Romans 10:10*

Here Paul explains that with the heart man believes (trusts), and with his mouth confession is made that the man can be saved (from harm). Surely there is no argument among believers today that redemptive salvation must be relative to a man's heart while if a man is in need of something he must pray. From this it can be plainly seen that the only requirement for man to be saved spiritually is trust while confession is needful to be saved physically.

Do not misunderstand. I am not preaching a universalistic theology. It is my contention that if a man truly does trust Christ he will be forced to change the way he lives. It is impossible to truly believe in God and not be affected thereby. The idea that circulates in pulpits that some men believe but are still not saved because they are unwilling to change is a lie. True belief is necessarily followed by repentance and life change.

Based on what we have just established, salvation cannot be accomplished by man even through prayer. At the same time, God is not capricious in his election of men. There must be trust/belief in the heart of a man in order for salvation to be accomplished. Still, the greatest argument for a works-based salvation stems from the Bible's teaching on baptism. Thus, for the remainder of this chapter we will discuss what the Bible teaches about this doctrine.

> ***"Now when they heard this, they were pricked in their heart, and said unto Peter and to the rest of the apostles, Men and brethren, what shall we do?***
> ***Then Peter said unto them, Repent, and be baptized every one of you in the name of Jesus Christ for the remission of sins, and ye shall receive the gift of the Holy Ghost."***
> ***(Acts 2:37,38)***

My father loved to tell the story of the little old preacher who would tell of this song when engaged in a discussion of baptism with those who believed in baptismal regeneration, "There is a fountain filled with blood drawn from Emmanuel's veins and sinners plunge beneath that flood lose all their guilty stains." He said, "It ought to be this way, there is a fountain filled with water drawn from the city main, and some folks plunge beneath that flood and go to hell Just the same."

So, let's begin to examine this one singular issue about which we must have an understanding. I want you know that whatever your denominational persuasion may be, I did not write this chapter to go church-bashing. The "Church of Christ" congregations often believe that baptism is essential for salvation and for that reason they might seem the subject of my discussion over the next few pages. I have no ill will toward the Church of Christ, and I believe that many of them are my family in the Lord. Whether or not they are justified believers depends not on their congregation's beliefs at large, rather it depends on what they are trusting. If baptism is what they are hoping will cleanse them of sin (as many of them do), then they are unfortunately not biblically saved, but if they look past the wonderful symbol of baptism to its deeper meaning and trust Jesus, then I am happy to call them brother or sister.

Max Lucado, perhaps the most well known member of the Church of Christ today, was speaking at a Church of Christ gathering in Nashville, Tennessee, when he was asked the question, "Do you believe that baptism is essential for salvation?" He responded, "No sir, I believe as the greater bulk of Christianity believes on that issue." At which point the crowd of Church of Christ preachers began to cheer.

I want you to know that there are many things that Church of Christ churches and mainstream conservative churches hold in common and, in fact, these areas of agreement are more plentiful than the differences. Thank God that Church of Christ churches agree that it is wrong to take the life of an unborn child by committing that sinful act of abortion. Former surgeon, General C. Everett Koop, said that in his thirty years in medicine he has "never seen one case where abortion was necessary to save a mother's life." Thank God that one thing that Church of Christ churches can agree upon is the truth that abortion is a grievous sin against an Almighty God.

All across this nation today there are men married to men thereby committing acts of sodomy, and women married to women who are committing acts of lesbianism. They assert that God in heaven has placed his seal of approval upon their relationship. Thank God that one thing that

Church of Christ congregations can agree upon is the truth that homosexuality is not acceptable in the eyes of the Lord.

The Churches of Christ churches are known for not allowing the use of musical instruments in their churches, but some of the instrumentalists and some of the singers I've seen in churches today almost make me want to agree with them because of flesh on parade. I have no problem with their contention, whether or not it has a biblical precedent. I want you to know that I have no desire to do harm to this congregation. They simply represent the belief in question.

The Who Of Baptism – Acts 2:38

The first thing that we need to discuss is the issue of who is supposed to be baptized. You say, "Well, Braxton, that's not the controversial stuff. That's not the stuff that we want to hear; we want to hear stuff we can fight about."

You know that's how we are, isn't it? We want to see the action packed part of everything; we want to see the bloody part of everything. Why do we watch ice-skating? "Oh, because it's so graceful." Oh, come on. Why do we really watch ice-skating? We want to see them fall and get humiliated in front of everyone. "Oh," you say, "I'm too spiritual for that." Ok, maybe you like to watch NASCAR. Why do we watch NASCAR? I've never met a man in my life who ever watched NASCAR just for the race. Why do we watch it? We want to see a crash. We want to see that Budweiser car get ripped to shreds at 250 mile per hour and then justify it by saying, "Well, we're against alcoholism." Why do we watch the discovery channel? It isn't to look at the pretty animals. We want to see that lion chase down that zebra and give him a few more stripes of a different color.

The problem is that we try to carry that with us into the Christian community and that's where the business meeting gets so popular. We know that Deacon Leroy is about to go after Brother Brown who's in charge of the men's bathroom. We're wasting money on double ply toilet paper and we want to see a fight. The Christian walk is one based on love. Put your guns away for a minute; you'll have your chance.

Who is to be baptized? The reason I start with this is simple. Before we talk about why people get baptized, or what baptism is or what kind of chlorine we should put in our baptistery, it must be understood to whom baptism should be applied. If my hypothesis is right and baptism is not an essential part of the salvation event, then why should anyone ever receive this holy rite of passage?

Let no mistake be made; this is the command given by God through Peter. Everyone on the face of the planet is commanded by the Father to (1) repent and (2) be baptized.

Baptism after repentance is a command. It doesn't matter what church you attend. It doesn't matter if you believe it's part of the salvation process or not. It doesn't matter if you think your hair is going to look nice after you come out. All believers are under a command from God to be baptized.

***"But when they believed Philip preaching the things concerning the kingdom of God, and the name of Jesus Christ, they were baptized, both men and women."* (Acts 8:12)**

Now, here we understand that this is not a sexist thing. This is not a chauvinistic thing, but rather this is a coed thing. Both men and women are to be baptized. I believe that one of the most beautiful sights that has ever entered my eyes is that of a married man and woman who came to know the Lord Jesus Christ together and were baptized at the same time.

However, every now and then you encounter a man who thinks that his wife ought to be more submissive than God ever intended. I recall hearing about a man who said, "My wife says she has repented and wants to be baptized, but preacher, I don't think she's ready. I'm not going to let her."

The preacher said, "I believe in male authority. That is the plan God has set forth, but when you go home, sir, you are in her territory where no one can help you, and either she gets baptized in water now or you're going to have a baptism of fire when you get home."

Who is to be baptized? Both men and women are.

Furthermore, I will tell you this, I also believe that because Christ said ". . . ***Suffer the little children to come unto me, and forbid them not: for of such is the kingdom of God." – Mark 10:14...*** if a child understands and has repented then a child, may also be baptized.

I want every parent to know that there is many a child today that is in danger of losing his eternal soul and finding himself in the lake of fire because some parent thinks that he is too young to make a decision.

I was preaching in a church not far from my home in McMinnville, Tennessee, one night, and it was one of those evenings when you could feel that you were about to experience a great movement of the Spirit. Throughout the entirety of the service there was a child on the back row seated between his mother and father. His eyes were pried wide open and fixed on me while hanging on every word that exited my lips. I want to tell you, I could look to one side and Grandpa Snagnasty on the front row had gone to sleep and had long since been snoring. On the other side was the song leader, and he was either asleep or doing some heavy praying. But on that back row, that sweet child was honed in on what God had to say. When the invitation came and the song was sung, that little boy indicated to me without a doubt that he wanted to make a decision for the Lord, yet when he tried to step out of the row, his mother and father both caught him by the arm and I could see there lips as they mouthed the words, "Sit back down."

Every week I see boys and girls who are young, but it is clear to me that they have as much an understanding of Jesus Christ, heaven and hell as half of most congregations do. Sadly, when it comes time for them to walk the aisle, mommy and daddy or grandma and grandpa stand in the way. Parents, you will have to answer for that on the day of judgment.

Who is to be baptized? All are to be baptized--man, woman, boy and girl. It is not an option; it is not a courtesy that you do Jesus or that you do a preacher. It is a commandment from the Almighty God.

The What Of Baptism

"Therefore we are buried with him by baptism into death: that like as Christ was raised up from the dead by the glory of the Father, even so we also should walk in newness of life." (Romans 6:4)

Now we understand who is to be baptized, but what is this strange ritual that has been set forth by Christ? Well, there are a few things that we must understand if we are going to define baptism. First of all, it depends on which baptism is being referred to.

"And I knew him not: but he that sent me to baptize with water, the same said unto me, Upon whom thou shalt see the Spirit descending, and remaining on him, the same is he which baptizeth with the Holy Ghost." (John 1:33)

I do not want to be accused of forcing my beliefs down anyone's throat. So, I want you to ask yourself a question. John says, "I'm baptizing with water; the Messiah is going to baptize with the Spirit." (paraphrase mine) How many baptisms is that, one or two? You can believe whatever you want to believe, but if you're going to believe what the Bible says, you've got to believe this way: the baptism that man performs is done in a physical way when a person is immersed in water while the baptism that Jesus performs is done in a spiritual way when a soul is immersed in the Holy Spirit.

If I go out and start mouthing off to a big group of angry, burly bikers in front of a bar I'm going to get absolutely beaten to a pulp. But if I, on the other hand, go home to my wife and mouth off to her, I may not get a physical beating but what I receive will be far worse than what those drunken bikers could produce.

This is what John is saying, "I can baptize you in water to show the decision that you have made and I can get you sopping wet in a physical way, but that baptism is nothing compared to the spiritual baptism that Jesus can perform." (paraphrase mine)

So, there are two baptisms. Do you believe that's what scripture says?

Now, because it's Jesus who saves and not a man like John, would you not say that when you are baptized with the Holy Ghost, as mentioned here, that it is in that moment when the holy Ghost comes upon you that you are saved? Answer me this. Can the Holy Ghost go to hell? Of course not. All right then, if a person has received the Holy Ghost, they are saved.

So, could we not then say that if a person has received the Holy Ghost, but has not yet been baptized in water, then water baptism, though an honorable thing, is not necessary for salvation? The answer is yes, we may. Moreover, this example occurs in scripture. ***"Can any man forbid water, that these should not be baptized, which have received the Holy Ghost as well as we? And he commanded them to be baptized in the name of the Lord. Then prayed they him to tarry certain days."*** (Acts 10:47,48)

The question has been asked, "Should we keep these men from being baptized who have already received the spirit." (paraphrase mine) This scripture clearly exemplifies that you get baptized with the spirit before you ever get baptized with water and that it's the baptism of the spirit that saves you.

Believing that the argument against the teaching of baptismal regeneration has been made, I could end this chapter now; however, we will now examine some of the more difficult verses about baptism and, by the way, this is where I'll probably offend somebody. Of course that doesn't really bother me anymore. Conservative Christians are considered offensive for a lot of reasons; PETA is after us because we like to eat meat and an animal had to die for that meat. Child services is after us because we spank our kids. So, why not be called offensive about baptism?

Let's see some tough verses.

> ***"For as many of you as have been baptized into Christ have put on Christ."*** **Galatians 3:27**

Well, what are we going to do now. That nails it down. We've got to be baptized into salvation. Remember, how many baptisms did John say there are? Now, look at verse 26.

> ***"For ye are all the children of God by faith in Christ Jesus."***

What is indicated here is that of the two baptisms mentioned, this one is a baptism by faith. Does that sound like the physical baptism or the spiritual one? This is the baptism of the Holy Spirit, not to be confused with the baptism of water.

Still not convinced? I'd like to point out another verse:

> ***"For by one Spirit are we all baptized into one body, whether we be Jews or Gentiles, whether we be bond or free; and have been all made to drink into one Spirit."*** **1 Corinthians 12:13**

Paul makes it clear that the way we are baptized into Christ, as he says in Galatians, is by the Spirit, not by water.

What about **1 Peter 3:20, 21**?

"Which sometime were disobedient, when once the longsuffering of God waited in the days of Noah, while the ark was a preparing, wherein few, that is, eight souls were saved by water. The like figure whereunto even baptism doth also now save us (not the putting away of the filth of the flesh, but the answer of a good conscience toward God,) by the resurrection of Jesus Christ:"

There it is. Noah was saved by water. That must mean that we've got to be baptized in water to be saved. Don't be foolish, my friend. Noah wasn't baptized with water. When it says that Noah was saved by water, it means that water cleansed the world of sin by drowning all the sinners. In fact, Peter says here "I'm not talking about that kind of baptism where you wash your dirt away with water; I'm talking about your conscience when you look to God and call on him to be saved." (paraphrase mine).

What about **Acts 2:38**?

> ***"Then Peter said unto them, Repent, and be baptized every one of you in the name of Jesus Christ for the remission of sins, and ye shall receive the gift of the Holy Ghost."***

How can we rationalize this? Now follow close. If I'm going to town for my wife, what does that mean I'm doing. It could mean I'm going to town to get something for her, or it could mean I'm going to town to get her. In the same way, this verse is often misunderstood to sound as if it's saying, " Repent and be baptized so that you can be saved," when, in actuality, it is saying, "Repent and be baptized because you've already gotten saved."

If all of that still does not convince you, then look with me at one final verse.:

> ***"For Christ sent me not to baptize, but to preach the gospel: not with wisdom of words, lest the cross of Christ should be made of none effect."*** **(I Corinthians 1:17)**

Paul said "I didn't come here to baptized I came here to preach the gospel." (paraphrase mine). What is the gospel? It is the good news of how we may be saved through Jesus Christ our Lord. Paul says here that baptism is not part of the gospel. Why? My friends, water baptism has got nothing to do with salvation taking place. It is merely a sign that you have been baptized in the spirit.

Years ago I was working near Lebanon, Tennessee, and I heard about a little girl whose grandfather had died. The family had prayed for years that the grandfather would be saved so that he could go to heaven. On the grand father's deathbed, the little girl crawled up and said, "Granddaddy, please accept Jesus. Please ask Jesus to save you!" He said, "You're right, sweetheart. I've wasted all these years. I want Jesus for my own." He prayed the sinner's prayer as his granddaughter led him. A few hours later he died. You and I know he was baptized in the Spirit, but because he wasn't baptized in water, the family was concerned. They went to the minister of the Church of Christ church and asked him, "Preacher we've got to know, is Granddaddy in heaven or hell." He knelt down to that little girl and said, "I'm sorry, sweetheart, your Grandfather is in hell tonight. He was never baptized."

You see friend, according to such a doctrine, the blood of Jesus Christ alone is not enough; Jesus is not enough, you've got to rely on something else. "My faith is built on nothing less than Jesus blood and righteousness. On Christ the solid rock I stand, all other ground is sinking sand . . . all other ground is sinking sand."

THE WHY OF BAPTISM

"Go ye therefore, and teach all nations, baptizing them in the name of the Father, and of the Son, and of the Holy Ghost:" **(Matt. 28:19)**

Why should we be baptized if it's not necessary for salvation? I'll tell you why, because Jesus commanded it. It is not a method by which you are saved, but it is an indication of your salvation. If you really have been saved, and really want to please the Lord, you'll gladly do the very first thing he asks of you and be baptized. There are many of you who would say, "Well, I got baptized when I was younger, but later on I really got saved. And I haven't been baptized since." You're living with an illegitimate baptism. You still haven't done the first thing Christ asks of you and you will never be blessed until you do. I have known of many people who have lived in misery, sickness and poverty because they did not do the very first thing that Christ asked. Today is your day to do something for Jesus.

Though I have focused the majority of this chapter on the subject of baptism, it is my intent to show that absolutely no physical ritual or effort is necessary for the actualization of salvation. Baptism was selected because most who would agree with my previous statement would still require this ordinance for salvation to take place. However, do not misunderstand. I am not diminishing the importance of baptism or other good works for the Christian. A saved life will be a changed life. Yet, this blinding light shows that the philosophy of works-based salvation is a farce.

Chapter 14: Understanding Predestination

In the mid 1980's the Southern Baptist Convention was nearly destroyed because the liberals and conservatives could not agree on issues such as the infallibility of the Bible. Everyone knew what the issues were and even the average lay church member could pretty well understand to what the topics amounted. It's becoming clear that in the days ahead, that convention and the entire realm of Christendom faces another such threat, but the devil has become more crafty. On whichever side of the argument you find yourself, there is a new issue that is threatening to divide our churches and the frightening thing is that most church members have little or no knowledge that this issue even exists; it is a debate over what is known as "Extreme Calvinism."

It should be said from the outset that these two chapters are somewhat out of place in a section regarding false doctrine. Though I believe that the view of the extreme Calvinist is false it is certainly not what may be viewed as a cult. Indeed if you are an extreme Calvinist and disagree with these two chapters it is imperative that you know my heart on this matter. I consider you to be a brother or sister in Christ. I recognize that many remarkable accomplishments of the faith can be attributed to extreme Calvinists and for that I admire and respect them. Nevertheless, this section may seem offensive in that I will explain why I see no logical reason to accept a certain area of Calvinistic theology.

Imagine with me that much of what you know about the Bible is wrong, but suddenly you became aware that God, before the foundation of the world, chose some people to go to heaven and there isn't anything they can do about it. Conversely, he chose some people to go to hell and there isn't anything they can do about it. In fact, many people are destined to go to hell and God is not even going to give them the chance to be saved. It doesn't matter how much they want it or how much they need it or how much they try to live for him, God created some people with the sole purpose of dying one day and going to hell. It would soon occur to you that you might be one of those who are not chosen. If you aren't chosen, there's no hope.

This is precisely what is believed by many Christians in the world today. This was the belief first of Augustine of Hippo hundreds, of years ago, but it has come to be known as Calvinism today because John Calvin of the reformation popularized it. Others call it the "Doctrine of Predestination" and many of those who hold it refer to it as the "Doctrine of Election."

Because some of my brothers in Christ believe this doctrine, I will try to remain as respectful as I can while still teaching the Bible, but for the next two chapters I will explain what the Bible really means by the verses in question and why the doctrine of election as the extreme Calvinist understands it is one of the greatest threats to God's church in the world today. It is daily destroying the faith of many would-be Christians. ***"For whom he did foreknow, he also did predestinate to be conformed to the image of his Son, that he might be the firstborn among many brethren. Moreover whom he did predestinate, them he also called: and whom he called, them he also justified: and whom he justified, them he also glorified."* - Romans 8:29,30**

First, we shall cut the head off of the dragon, so to speak. The passage of scripture that is most commonly used to defend the doctrine of extreme Calvinism is that of Romans 8:29, 30. After all, look at it. How can we get around this, it says that he predestined people. No reason to go any further, we're sunk. The idea of the extreme Calvinist wins out. Now before I say anything that upsets you, I want to explain again that I don't think we ought to let this issue divide us.

The story is told of a group of theologians who were discussing the tension between predestination and free will. Things became so heated that the group broke up into two opposing factions. But one man, not knowing which to join, stood for a moment trying to decide. At last he joined the predestination group. "Who sent you here?" they asked. "No one sent me," he replied. "I came of my own free will." "Free will!" they exclaimed. "You can't join us! You belong with the other group!" So he followed their orders and went to the other clique. There someone asked, "When did you decide to join us?" The young man replied, "Well, I didn't really decide--I was sent here." "Sent here!" they shouted. "You can't join us unless you have decided by your own free will!"

What a silly reason to divide the family of God. Still, I will be speaking frankly about the issue at hand regardless of how it may alienate some readers. The truth must be exposed.

What you've got to understand about this passage is that it means exactly what it says, but you can't bring your own ideas to the passage. You must let the passage speak for itself. The reason many who believe in baptismal regeneration believe it is because they bring their own presuppositions to Acts 2:38 and unpack them, rather than letting it speak for itself as it is read.

We will begin by defining some of the words in this passage. Consider the word , "foreknow." What does it mean to foreknow something? Well, the extreme Calvinist would explain that if God foreknew something, then it means he made it happen; it was predestined. This is wrong for two reasons.

1. It's wrong for if foreknowledge means the same thing as predestined, then God makes no sense to say the same word twice in the same sentence. That is to say, if foreknowledge is the same as predestination, then the verse reads, "For whom he did predestinate, he also did predestinate. . ." Does that make any sense?

2. There is no point in making up a definition for foreknowledge when it already means simply, "to know before," or "to have prior knowledge of."

I like to explain foreknowledge this way. If I read the last page of a book, and then I go back and start reading chapter one, I have foreknowledge of how the book will end. I have "prior knowledge of." But does it mean that I wrote the book? That's ridiculous.

I know my mail man comes by my house at 1:00 in the afternoon to deliver the mail. So, when I wake up, I have foreknowledge about when he's probably going to be there. Does that mean I made it happen? I just knew before. I foreknew.

Let me give you another one. I estimated this morning that I have seen the movie, Star Wars, nearly three hundred times, because when I was eight, nine and ten years old I watched it every day in the summer. Since there are about ninety days in a summer and I saw it for three summers plus at least thirty other times throughout my life, I would say I have seen it three hundred times. You know, I have seen it a lot. I know how the story ends. I could probably quote a good portion of the movie to you. When we sit down to watch Star Wars, I've got a lot of foreknowledge about what's going to happen. Now, does that mean I wrote, directed and produced Star Wars. I wish that I had; I would be a wealthy man today.

Foreknowledge means exactly what you would think--fore-knowledge. Now despite all of this, the extreme Calvinist might say that in the Greek it is conceivable that it could possibly if you cross your fingers click your heels together and use your imagination mean God predestined things, but even if that were so, there are many words that God could have used that would have clearly indicated that. Foreknowledge means "to know before."

Then it says, "Those he foreknew he did predestinate. . ." It is often assumed that the word "predestinate" refers to salvation. But that's not what the passage says. Read the rest, ". . . to be conformed into the image of his Son." Predestination does not refer to someone getting saved; it refers to someone who already is saved. What is predestined is that if you become a Christian, it is predetermined that you will become like Christ. When I explain this to extreme Calvinists, they, without exception say to me, "Well, in other scriptures where predestination is mentioned, it refers to salvation." That's interesting.

Extreme Calvinists seem to believe that the word predestination is found in every nook and cranny in the Bible. It might surprise you to know that predestination and all its derivatives are only mentioned in four verses. In Ephesians 1:5, 11, it explains that people who are saved are predestined to become part of God's family and to get his inheritance.

"Having predestinated us unto the adoption of children by Jesus Christ to himself, according to the good pleasure of his will,

In whom also we have obtained an inheritance, being predestinated according to the purpose of

him who worketh all things after the counsel of his own will:

We've already talked about what predestination means in Romans 8:29,30. No one who really studies this without bringing their own beliefs to the passage would understand it to say that predestination has to do with salvation; it never has. It has to do with what is going to happen to a person after they are saved.

This is one of the most commonly misunderstood passages of scripture. But you see, if you just plainly read the Bible for what it says, you won't have the problems that the extreme Calvinist does.

There is a church that many years ago split over this very idea. Every year at the church's annual picnic one of the deacons who was a Calvinist would stand up and hold his chicken leg in the air and say, "I was predestined before the foundation of the earth to eat this chicken leg," and he would take a bite. One year, when he stood and said that, another deacon grabbed it out of his hand and said, "No you weren't," and he ate it and the church split. I mean we split over some silly things.

But what you must understand is that what God has predestined is that if you become a Christian, you will become like Christ and you don't have any choice about that. But whether or not you become a Christian is up to you; God has chosen you. Will you choose him in return? God has elected you, will you respond to that election?

Jacob And Esau

"(For the children being not yet born, neither having done any good or evil, that the purpose of God according to election might stand, not of works, but of him that calleth;) It was said unto her, The elder shall serve the younger. As it is written, Jacob have I loved, but Esau have I hated." - Romans 9:11-13

Here is where we come to another area of difficulty, because it says that before Jacob or Esau ever did anything good or evil, God had decided to love Jacob and hate Esau. Now once again we look at this and say, "Huh, there it is. God does predestine some for salvation and some for hell." But I want you to remember some things here.

1. Love and hate meant different things in the scripture than when we use them today. Biblically, love and hate are actions rather than feelings. If I do harm to someone, I am hating them, because hate is an action. If I do well to someone, I am treating them with love. It is absolutely unbiblical to believe

anything that Jesus said about love and not accept that love and hate are actions, not feelings or states of mind. So, what God is saying when he says, "Jacob have I loved and Esau have I hated," is actually, "I'm going to make Jacob successful and I'm going to make Esau fail. I'm going to do well by Jacob and I'm going to do harm to Esau."

2. Salvation is not mentioned here. If you say that this has anything to do with salvation, you are only reading into scripture something that is not there to promote your own ideas. Calvin himself said, "To speak on predestination where the Bible does not is no more sensible that attempting to see in darkness."[1]

3. Scripture is clear, that God is not speaking of the individuals Jacob and Esau but the nations that came out of them. Do you see where it says, "As it is written, Jacob have I loved but Esau have I hated"? Well, where was that written? It was written in Malachi 1:2, 3.

"I have loved you, saith the LORD. Yet ye say, Wherein hast thou loved us? Was not Esau Jacob's brother? saith the LORD: yet

I loved Jacob, And I hated Esau, and laid his mountains and his heritage waste for the dragons of the wilderness."

In Malachi 1:2-3, it explains how God hated Esau, and how does it say he hated him? "Laid his mountains and his heritage to waste for the dragons of the wilderness." In fact, just so there's no confusion, Malachi takes it a step further and uses the name, "Edom," the nation that came out of Esau. Moreover, if after all of that you're still confused, consider Genesis 25:23:

"And the LORD said unto her, Two nations are in thy womb, and two manner of people shall be separated from thy bowels; and the one people shall be stronger than the other people; and the elder shall serve the younger.. And God always called his people Israel which was Jacob."

4. It is never said here that Esau's nation couldn't have won God's favor if they had become a righteous nation.

But of all four of the reasons that I have given that show that this passage does not support the ideas of the extreme Calvinist, the preeminent one is simply that it doesn't even speak of salvation one way or the other. That is simply read into the text.

Women rarely mean what they say when they say that nothing is bothering them. What a wife really means is that her husband didn't realize that she cut three inches off her hair, and since he didn't realize that, he obviously doesn't care about her, and if he doesn't care about her, he must not care about the kids either because she gave birth to them, and so the whole marriage is a sham. Did he say any of those things? Of course not. Now, to take it a step further. If he says, " Wait a minute, I didn't say that."

She will then reply, "Well, you didn't have to say it. I knew what you were what thinking."

In the same way some extreme Calvinists look at a passage like this and begin to unpack their own theology because they have already decided what is right with very little regard for what the passage is really saying. When asked whether the passage actually said all that, the extreme Calvinist may respond, "It doesn't have to; I know what it means." In this way he attempts to know and understand the mind of Christ with completeness. For reasons such as this, extreme Calvinism is an elitist theology.

It is also elitist because it supposes that God values some more than others. He offers salvation to some and damns others. Scripture plainly says that God is not a respecter of persons (Acts 10:34). The

Calvinist will say that God does not love everyone, but only those he chooses. When scripture says:

> *"For God so loved the world, that he gave his only begotten Son, that whosoever believeth in him should not perish, but have everlasting life." - John 3:16.*

Calvinism says only a select few will enter heaven and you can't even cry out for mercy from God when scripture says in 1 Tim. 2:4, *"**Who will have all men to be saved, and to come unto the knowledge of the truth. For there is one God, and one mediator between God and men, the man Christ Jesus; Who gave himself a ransom for all, to be testified in due time.**"*

PHARAOH

*"**What shall we say then? Is there unrighteousness with God? God forbid. For he saith to Moses, I will have mercy on whom I will have mercy, and I will have compassion on whom I will have compassion. So then it is not of him that willeth, nor of him that runneth, but of God that sheweth mercy. For the scripture saith unto Pharaoh, Even for this same purpose have I raised thee up, that I might shew my power in thee, and that**"*

***my name might be declared throughout all the earth. Therefore hath he mercy on whom he will have mercy, and whom he will he hardeneth."* - Romans 9:14-18**

A final consideration for our discussion is what is said of Pharaoh. How can we get around this one? It says God raised Pharaoh up for this purpose and hardened his heart.

1. First of all, look at the phrase, "raised you up." The extreme Calvinist would have you believe that it means that God created Pharaoh and raised him up as a child to this point in his life for this purpose. Yet, "raised up" is used in scripture to mean, "made powerful." The evidence of this is (Jeremiah 51:11, Isaiah 41:2, 2 Samuel 23:1, Judges 2:16). So, what I want you to see is that Pharaoh was not born for this purpose, but at some point, God made him particularly powerful for this purpose.

2. Second, the Calvinist would point out that God hardened Pharaoh's heart so that he couldn't be saved. Fine, God did harden Pharaoh's heart that he couldn't become a believer, but not before Pharaoh had turned

God down and turned away from God. Consider the following scripture:

"And Pharaoh hardened his heart at this time also, neither would he let the people go." - Exodus 8:32
"And when Pharaoh saw that the rain and the hail and the thunders were ceased, he sinned yet more, and hardened his heart, he and his servants." - Exodus 9:34

Pharaoh hardened his own heart, and then in Chapter 10, God hardened his heart. I've preached many times that you can hear the message, know that God is trying to reach you and you can harden your heart and walk out without being saved. Perhaps you might return to church again, and God once more draws on you and indeed drags you to the point of salvation, but you harden your heart. Finally, according to Proverbs 1:24, God will eventually be done with you. He says:

"Because I have called, and ye refused; I have stretched out my hand, and no man regarded; But ye have set at nought all my counsel, and would none of my reproof: I also will laugh at your calamity; I will mock when your fear cometh; When your fear cometh as desolation, and your destruction cometh

as a whirlwind; when distress and anguish cometh upon you. Then shall they call upon me, but I will not answer; they shall seek me early, but they shall not find me: For that they hated knowledge, and did not choose the fear of the LORD: They would none of my counsel: they despised all my reproof."
   - Proverbs 1:24-30

You might say, "Do you believe that Pharaoh could have been saved?" At one time in his life, I believe Pharaoh could have said, "God I realize that I've hardened my own heart and I have turned away from you, but I'm going to treat your people well and I'm going to love you and I want to be your servant!" Yes, I believe God would have forgiven him. Otherwise, the Bible is a book of lies for God would not be a God of love.

Friend, I want you to step back from this thing for a moment and think about it, not with the worldly wisdom that often gets us in trouble, but with your heart. If God created certain people so that they would go to hell without any possibility of being saved, is God really a God of love? If God says in John 3:16 that he loves the whole world but yet sends some of those he claims to love to hell without the possibility of salvation, is he a God of Love?

I have heard it rationalized this way: The extreme Calvinist will say, "Yes, God is a God of mercy because he saves some when he doesn't have to save any." They will use an illustration by saying, "What if a farmer had a pond and on that pond he had a sign that said 'no swimming,' but three boys ignored his law and swam anyway. If he decides to save two of them and let one drown, "…then he," the extreme Calvinists say, "should be considered a merciful man because he put the sign up, he warned them and they didn't heed the warning. He didn't have to save any. So, since he didn't have to save any, if he saved two and let one drown, he is still a merciful and loving farmer."

May I say to you that if that farmer could have saved all three but let one drown, there is not a person in the world who would consider him merciful. In truth, he could be tried for negligent homicide. On the other hand, if he offers the drowning boy a chance to live and throws him a line with an attached life preserver, and the boy still turns away and drowns regardless, that is a merciful farmer indeed.

If God claims to love all of mankind but offers only some salvation, he is a negligent and uncaring, unmerciful beast of a God. But if he offers salvation and it is rejected, he can rightly be called loving.

[1] Calvin, John. ***Institutes of the Christian Faith***

Chapter 15: Examining the Tulip

In the mid nineties there was a terrible story about a mother who looked like a wonderful lady. She would have fit in on any Nick at Nite television program as the darling mother/housewife. She was affectionate, she cared for her children she seemed to love them and worked hard for her family. One day as she was riding down the road with her two boys in the back seat of the car, she became frustrated by their constant whining and fussing and she warned them to be quiet and sit still or else there would be punishment. They continued and she warned them again. Still, they continued and they received their punishment. Little did they know that their mother was about to punish them by getting out of the car, leaving them inside, placing the car in neutral and pushing it into a pond where both boys drowned.

I want to ask you in all sincerity, could anyone say about this woman that she was a model mother and a loving one? Of course not, she went to prison, and she is hated by the world for her actions.

Yet, there is the doctrine of extreme Calvinism that says God warned the whole world of sin but they disregarded that warning so the punishment is hell. In other words, because God warned man, he is well within his rights to send us all to hell without question. He decides to save some, and Calvinism teaches that some he decided would end up in hell with no way to call on him for salvation, and they can not be saved. Others he has predestined to go to heaven, and whether they like it or not, that's where they are going. Now, suppose that mother had allowed one of those children to live and only killed the other. Would she be considered merciful? Of course not, but God is considered merciful by the Calvinist when he restricts salvation to only a few that he predetermines.

In the words of Adrian Rogers, "If you believe that kind of thing, you've got a screw loose somewhere." In this chapter I am going to deconstruct the famous extreme Calvinist argument known as the TULIP in such a way that Logic will prevail and readers will arrive at the blinding light of free will.

TOTAL DEPRAVITY

"There is none that understandeth, there is none that seeketh after God". **Romans 3:11**

Scripture clearly teaches that man is totally depraved. That is to say, he is completely sinful. In fact, he is completely sinful from before his birth as King David said of himself that he was a sinner in his mother's womb. For this reason, we all need a savior. The extreme Calvinist believes all of that and it's true. But when the extreme Calvinist says total depravity, what he really means is total inability. They mean that verses like this one actually teach that man is completely unable to call on God, so man never would. Not only does this make no sense in light of the whosoevers in scripture, it's not what the phrase "total depravity" even means. Depravity (not a biblical term) comes from the Greek word, "deprever," which means crooked. Thus, to be totally depraved means totally crooked, but not totally unable.

Let me explain it like this. The other day I tried to wash some clothes--mistake number one. I got all the stuff separated between lights and darks and all that kind of thing. I knew that much, but when it came down to doing the loads, I put it on some kind of weird cycle, and I put the dryer sheets in the washing machine. Male readers are probably thinking, "What's wrong with that?" I put some detergent in the dryer, and when I got it all out, I did the most terrible job of ironing you've ever seen. I did five loads that way. I've got news for you. I was totally depraved. I was totally crooked. I was not doing well at all. But you know, I could still call out to my wife for help.

When I was in algebra two, I was totally depraved. I had enough trouble handling numbers on their own without "x" and "y" and "a" and "b." Then you get to imaginary numbers. Imaginary numbers? Is it not hard enough? Now you've got to go adding things that don't even exist. I was told I would need that mess. I have never needed it or used it. In fact, I still can't write the letters "x" and "y" without getting angry. I was totally crooked and depraved, but I could still call out to my teacher for help.

What scriptures like this teach is total depravity, total crookedness, total sinfulness, but not total inability. Man, though he's sinful, can still call on God to save him.

The extreme Calvinist will say, "But doesn't the Bible say that men are dead in sin, and so they can't do good things because they are dead." Adam and Eve realized their sinfulness and were ashamed. They sought means to make it right before God even came to them.

> *"And the eyes of them both were opened, and they knew that they were naked; and they sewed fig leaves together, and made themselves aprons." - Genesis 3:7*

Moreover, they'll use Matt. 7:17-18 about good trees producing good fruit and bad trees producing bad fruit to show that if you are a bad tree you will never produce good fruit and if you are a good tree you will never produce bad fruit. One problem with that is good trees sometime do produce bad fruit and, in the same way, bad trees can sometimes produce good fruit.

In other words, bad people can sometimes do good things, and one thing they can do is realize their totally depraved and totally crooked state and call on God to save them. He will answer.

> *"But now he commandeth all men everywhere to repent."* (Acts 17:30) *"come unto me all ye who are heavy laden and I will give you rest."* (Matt. 11:28) *"and the spirit of the bride say come, let him hears say come let him who thirsts say come, and whosoever will let him take of the water of life freely".* (Rev. 22:17)

Unconditional Election

"For whom he did foreknow, he also did predestinate to be conformed to the image of his Son, that he might be the firstborn among many brethren." **(Romans 8:29)**

In brief, unconditional election is the idea that God before the foundation of the world chose some for salvation and some for hell despite what they may want.

Laurence M. Vance said, "If all one ever listened to were Calvinists, one would think the entire Bible revolved around unconditional election."[1]

I don't know how many homosexuals you've been around, but they function somewhat the same way. In their estimation, their life is all about the fact that they are gay. That's all that matters to many of them. Every conversation they have is ultimately about the fact that they are gay. Some are the same way about their race. Everything has to do with the fact that they are of a particular people group or minority.

Extreme Calvinists are many times that way. Everything goes back to this one thing they believe, and when people get turned off by them because this is all they talk about, they justify it by saying, "Well they must not be one of the elect." Ultimately, many extreme Calvinists believe that the only people who are truly elect are others who embrace extreme Calvinism.

Unconditional election was dealt with extensively in the first section of this chapter and thus I will not spend much more time debunking the idea now. However, I want to add to this that Judges 5:2 says that people, "***willingly offered themselves***"1 Chronicles 28:9 says David encouraged Solomon to serve God with a "***willful mind***" 1 Corinthians 9:17 says, "***For if I do this thing willingly I have a reward.***"

Moreover, there are a great many passages in scripture which conflict with the extreme view of sovereignty held by the extreme Calvinist. If God's will is done despite the decisions of man, why does God so often claim that his will has not been done?

> "***The Lord is not slack concerning his promise, as some men count slackness; but is longsuffering to us-ward, not willing that any should perish, but that all should come to repentance.***" – *2 peter 3:9*
>
> "***O Jerusalem, Jerusalem, thou that killest the prophets, and stonest them which are sent unto thee, how often would I have gathered thy children together, even as a hen gathereth her chickens under her wings, and ye would not!***" – *Matthew 23:37*

> *"Say unto them, As I live, saith the Lord GOD, I have no pleasure in the death of the wicked; but that the wicked turn from his way and live: turn ye, turn ye from your evil ways; for why will ye die, O house of Israel?"*
> *- Ezekiel 33:11*

Even in some passages it is indicated that if man would turn to righteousness, God would forgive.

> *"Therefore I will judge you, O house of Israel, every one according to his ways, saith the Lord GOD. Repent, and turn yourselves from all your transgressions; so iniquity shall not be your ruin." – Ezekiel 18:30*

LIMITED ATONEMENT

> *"Christ hath redeemed us from the curse of the law, being made a curse for us: for it is written, Cursed is every one that hangeth on a tree:"* **(Gal. 3:13)**

This verse is meant to help support the idea of limited atonement. That is to say, Christ's death on the cross only was sufficient to cover a certain number of sinners. Frankly, this and other verses supporting limited atonement can be seen by non-Calvinists as a simple statement about the gospel. This area of extreme Calvinistic theology is a glaring example of imported beliefs. Moreover, the idea that God wanted to save all men, as argued a moment ago, but only saved a few makes for a pretty puny God. Christ's death on the cross was a pure enough sacrifice to cover all the sins of the world. And he's a big enough God to do it.

John Eldridge wrote in his book, Wild At Heart, about a time he went bear hunting in Alaska. He saw claw marks all over the trees, fish guts everywhere and droppings from that bear as big as dogs. Then he saw that monstrosity. At two stories tall, he said that he thought that thing could rip him apart. Remember, God said about that bear that it is good. God goes to the extreme. He's a big enough God to save the whole world. [2]

A well known Southern Baptist theologian argued at the Southern Baptist Convention in 2006 that every conservative Christian believes in limited atonement to some degree in that not everyone is saved. Raising a straw man, the speaker made a worthless point. Yet, if extreme Calvinists insist that this truth proves some sort of limited atonement, it is as far as we may follow them. There is no biblical basis for selective limited atonement.

IRRESISTIBLE GRACE

"The LORD of hosts hath sworn, saying, Surely as I have thought, so shall it come to

***pass; and as I have purposed, so shall it stand:* (Isaiah 14:24)**

From this verse and others like it is built the doctrine of Irresistible Grace. Simply stated, it is the idea that God must call certain people to heaven and certain people to hell, because if God's grace was free to everyone, no one would resist it.

Let me say that my wife is irresistible to me. But even before I met my wife, women were irresistible to me. How many of you men would agree that women are irresistible? But I wanted a woman from the moment I saw one. I thought, "Wow! It sure would be nice to have a woman." I started looking for one. It never occurred to me that I might not need one. I never had to wonder, "Am I attracted to them." I'm what God intended in a man—a Christian, redblooded, conservative, heterosexual, Bible-believing fanatic. And when I saw Sarah, she was so irresistible I said, "Whooooooooo! She's hot!"

Here is the difference. Women, (like Sarah), were irresistible to me because I had seen them with my own eyes. God doesn't reveal himself to man that way so that it is possible for them to make an objective choice and ask, "Will I believe or not?" I agree that if his grace could be seen with human eyes, it would be irresistible. This is why

Jesus said to Thomas, "You believe because you saw, but blessed is he that believes and has not seen."

Perseverance of the Saints

The perseverance of the saints speaks of the duty of the elected believer to persevere and keep the faith (or prove that he has the faith), but this works entirely against eternal security. If a believer has the task of persevering in the faith and might fail, then he was not unconditionally elected. Though the extreme Calvinist would never agree, this is a works-based salvation.

This entire system of theology is one of arrogant elitism that teaches that God is partial, biased and unjust because he picks some for salvation and others for hell without even offering them the forgiveness that he preaches. The extreme Calvinist seems to believe in a cruel God.

Take a step back from this thing and do what I asked at the end of the last chapter. Look at it with your heart. Is it a loving God who would create some people for the sole purpose of going to hell, or does that undermine the entire faith? Isn't that a God who is more like the woman who drowned her two boys in the car for being too loud without offering them forgiveness?

There is one question that I have asked of extreme Calvinists everywhere and they cannot answer. Do people that go to hell deserve to go there? Because if they were not offered grace so that they could become clean, why should they be blamed for being dirty.

I have had a wonderful father all my life. He has always treated me justly. I broke his rules a lot, and I would get punished sometimes. Still, my father offered me grace and forgiveness. Regardless of what I had done, he still loved me and forgave me. My father has a lot of love for me. If I am to believe extreme Calvinism, I must believe that though God's love for me far outweighs the love my father could have, my father would forgive me but God would not. Unfortunately, the God of extreme Calvinism is one who claims to love beyond all others but in the end is full of venomous lies as he sends his lover to eternal separation.

[1] Vance, Lawrence M. ***The Other Side of Calvinism***. Vance Publications.

[2] Eldredge, John. ***Wild At Heart***. Thomas Nelson.

SECTION 4

Having now established that there is a God, that Jesus is God, and which version of Jesus is God, we have shown the blinding lights of Christian theism. One thing remains. Now that Christian theism is accepted, what can we know for sure about our own salvation? This final section is devoted to what we can know for certain about the Christian life. If you have not yet begun that relationship, then you may consider the prerequisite for this chapter a conversion experience. Simply trust Christ for salvation, repent (turn) from your sin, and tell God in prayer that you want to be cleansed and begin a life with Him. As already demonstrated, that trust and belief is all that is required. For those who have just taken that monumental step, the first chapter of this section is present to help you understand the blinding lights that should be present in your own life if you truly are now a believer.

Chapter 16: The Blinding Lights of a Believer

"These things have I written unto you that believe on the name of the Son of God; that ye may know that ye have eternal life, and that ye may believe on the name of the Son of God." -1 John 5:13

You know, if there's one thing that we need if we're going to get by in today's world, it's knowledge. I don't know how many times I have heard people say, "Knowledge is power." When they were children, some went to school for just a few years and then started to work. Some went to school for twelve years and then began to work, but now, if we want to be sure a kid is going to survive out there, we've got to at least put him through twelve years and then send him through four more years of college. He might have to go through even more than that. For our own survival, we must know things.

One of the things that I love about children is that they don't know anything. We once kept a little boy for one week, but you could spend five seconds with that boy and you'd realize how much he didn't know. All he really knew was that he wanted to go swimming all the time. We'd be in the car, and he'd point at the gas meter and say "Why's that there?"

I'd say, "That tells you how much gas is in the car."

"Why?" He asked.

I responded, "So we know how much farther we can go on the gas we've got."

"Why?"

My reply was, "So we can get to where we're going."

Not to be daunted, he would ask, "Where we going?"

I said, "To the store."

Naturally, he asked, "Why we going there?"

Ready to surrender I said, "Because we've got to get something there!"

Then he always ended by asking, "If there's a pool there, can we go swimming?" It's amazing how much he doesn't know. You've got to know things if you're going to make it today.

Moreover, because of all the liars and faithless people out there, we haven't just got to know things, we've got to know them for certain. Things must be proven to us. We've got to see it and have pictures if we're going to believe.

That's what I like about what John does in his first epistle. He tells us the things that we can know for certain about Christianity.

As we begin talking about what we as Christians can know for certain about the Bible and about our faith, I want you to know that the Devil is going to try his hardest to make sure that you doubt these things. Every believer has doubts from time to time, but that doesn't mean there is insufficient evidence for faith. Most married couples doubt the love their spouse has for them from time to time. It's not that they don't have sufficient evidence of that love, it might just be that they haven't spent enough time in the company of their lover. I submit to you that in your times of doubt you were probably not reading the Bible as you should.

G. Campbell Morgan had already enjoyed some success as a preacher by the time he was 19 years old, but then he was attacked by doubts about the Bible. The writings of various scientists and agnostics disturbed him (e.g., Charles Darwin, John Tyndall, Thomas Huxley, and Herbert Spencer). As he read their books and listened to debates, Morgan became more and more perplexed. What did he do?

He cancelled all preaching engagements, put all the books in a cupboard, locked the door, went to the bookstore and bought a new Bible. He said to himself, "I am no longer sure that this is what my father claims it to be--the Word of God. But of this I am sure. If it be the Word of God, and if I come to it with an unprejudiced and open mind, it will bring assurance to my soul of itself." The result? "That Bible found me!" said Morgan. The new assurance in 1883 gave him the motivation for his preaching and teaching ministry. He devoted himself to the study and preaching of God's Word.[1]

Just reading God's word will bring assurance to your heart. Remember that in a time of doubt.

OBEY

"And hereby we do know that we know him, if we keep his commandments. He that saith, I know him, and keepeth not his commandments, is a liar, and the truth is not in him. But whoso keepeth his word, in him verily is the love of God perfected: hereby know we that we are in him."
– 1 John 2:3-5

The Bible says that the number one way that you can know for sure if you are saved is if you are obeying God.

It is said that on his retreat from Greece after his great military expedition there, King Xerxes boarded a Phoenician ship along with a number of his Persian troops. But a fearful storm came up, and the captain told Xerxes there was no hope unless the ship's load was substantially lightened. The king turned to his fellow Persians on deck and said, "It is on you that my safety depends. Now let some of you show your regard for your king." A number of the men bowed to Xerxes and threw themselves overboard! Lightened of its load, the ship made it safely to harbor. Xerxes immediately ordered that a golden crown be given to the pilot for preserving the king's life -- then ordered the man beheaded for causing the loss of so many Persian lives![1]

The Bible says that the number one way that we can know if were saved for certain is if we are obeying God. You know why we doubt our faith? It's because we aren't obeying God. We know that we know him because we keep his commandments.

And the proof of that is this: those that are the most sure and have the most peace and are calm when they die are those people who serve him as much as they can. I believe there are a lot of us who obey God by doing the bare minimum, and one day in heaven we're going to feel like Xerxes' captain. A crown will be placed on our heads, a victory will be won, but we really didn't do the best that we could have done.

The way to keep from doubting is to obey the word of God.

I'm not pulling this out of thin air. John is so passionate that we receive this message that in verse 29 he says it again. Here John says it another way. He says, "What do we know for certain about Jesus; we know that he's righteous." Well, if we know that he's righteous, doesn't it make sense that people that are righteous are born of him?

When the pastor's conference was happening at First Baptist Church in downtown Jacksonville, Florida, I had some free time with nothing to do so I thought I'd go into the women's conference. I mean, after all, Homer Lindsey's wife was going to be leading it, and I wanted to hear her. I went in and sat on the back row. I learned all about how to be a wonderful Christian wife for my husband. I just had a wonderful time. But at the end as we got up to leave, a lady looked at me and said, "What are you doing here?"

I said, "I came to hear Mrs. Lindsey."

Then she made a brilliant observation when she said, "But you're a man."

And I said "What ever gave you that idea?"

Well what *had* given her that idea? She knew what men generally looked like; she saw short hair and a necktie and she thought, "Looks like a man, dresses like a man, smells like a man, it must be a man."

You might say, "Well, it's simple to tell the difference between a man and a woman." Sometimes it's not. But, hey, it's just as easy to tell the difference between righteousness and unrighteousness for a saved person. What does John say we know for certain? He says that we know that Jesus is righteous. So, if you know what a righteous person looks like, ask yourself, "Do I look righteous, act righteous, dress righteous and smell righteous just like Jesus?" If so, you know you are born of Jesus. How can you be sure you're saved? John says you can know you're saved if you keep his commandments.

LOVE

"We know that we have passed from death unto life, because we love the brethren. He that loveth not his brother abideth in death." - 1 John 3:14

The number one way that you can know that you are saved is by observing yourself obeying God, but the second way that John gives you to know that you are saved is that when you are saved, you love people whom you didn't love before.

The Bible affirms that when it says that you'll know you are saved if you love people when you didn't love them before. ***"My little children, let us not love in word, neither in tongue; but in deed and in truth. And hereby we know that we are***

of the truth, and shall assure our hearts before him." – 1 John 3:18-19

But what if you can't love someone? What if someone has hurt you so deeply that the amount of baggage over which you must climb to forgive and love them seems insurmountable? Treat them with love, regardless. Do that and you will find yourself loving them.

Newspaper columnist and minister, George Crane, tells of a wife who came into his office full of hatred toward her husband. "I do not only want to get rid of him, I want to get even. Before I divorce him, I want to hurt him as much as he has hurt me."

Dr. Crane suggested an ingenious plan. He said, "Go home and act as if you really love your husband. Tell him how much he means to you. Praise him for every decent trait. Go out of your way to be as kind, considerate, and generous as possible. Spare no efforts to please him, to enjoy him. Make him believe you love him. After you've convinced him of your undying love and that you cannot live without him, then drop the bomb. Tell him that you're getting a divorce. That will really hurt him."

With revenge in her eyes, she smiled and exclaimed, "Beautiful, beautiful. Will he ever be surprised!" And she did it with enthusiasm. Acting "as if." for two months, she showed love, kindness, listening, giving, reinforcing, and sharing.

When she didn't return, Crane called. "Are you ready now to go through with the divorce?"

"Divorce?" she exclaimed. "Never! I discovered I really do love him." Her actions had changed her feelings. Motion resulted in emotion. The ability to love is established not so much by fervent promise as often repeated deeds.[1]

How can you know that you are saved? Start loving people. Though it may sound like a pointless question, how can you know if you're loving people?

"By this we know that we love the children of God, when we love God, and keep his commandments." -1 John 5:2

Here John ties these two things together. He says, "You know that you love God's people when you find yourself loving God by keeping his commandments."

SPIRIT

"And he that keepeth his commandments dwelleth in him, and he in him. And hereby we know that he abideth in us, by the Spirit which he hath given us." – 1 John 3:24

Finally, John says there's one more way that you can know that you're saved. You can know that you're saved if you've got the Holy Spirit inside of you. You say, "Well, I think I've got the Holy Spirit inside of me, but I just don't know." John explains it for us:

"Hereby know ye the Spirit of God: Every spirit that confesseth that Jesus Christ is come in the flesh is of God:" - 1 John 4:2

He says the way you know that you have the Spirit is if you are compelled to tell others about Jesus. I've got to tell you, when I'm around people who are lost, I can't think about anything except that if they died they would be in hell. For that reason, I am compelled to tell others about Jesus.

It's because of the Spirit that's inside of me. You know that you're saved because of the Spirit and you know that you have the Spirit because he compels you to tell others about Jesus.

After John Wesley had been preaching for some time, someone said to him, "Are you sure, Mr. Wesley, of your salvation?"

"Well," he answered, "Jesus Christ died for the whole world."

"Yes, we all believe that; but are you sure that you are saved?"

Wesley replied that he was sure that the provision had been made for his salvation.

"But are you sure, Wesley, that you are saved?"

It went like an arrow to his heart, and he had no rest or power until that question was settled. Many men and many women go on month after month, and year after year, without power, because they do not know their standing in Christ; they are not sure of their own footing for eternity. Latimer wrote Ridley once that when he was settled and steadfast about his own salvation, he was as bold as a lion; but if that hope became eclipsed, he was fearful and afraid and was disqualified for service. Many are disqualified for service because they are continually doubting their own salvation.[1]

When I was a teenager, I got so scared one Sunday listening to the preacher that I felt I would lose my mind. Afterwards, I asked him how I could know I was saved, and he said the same thing John said, "Are you obeying God? Are you loving others? Are you compelled by the Spirit?"

Let me put it in language we can understand. Ask your self three questions: (1) Do I want to please God? (2) Do I love God's people, fellowshipping with them like a family? (3) Do I have a desire to see people saved? If those three things are true, then you can be sure that you are a child of God.

We know all of this is true because John makes this argument with things we know for certain;

things we are sure of. But there is one more thing that John says that we know for sure.

> ***"And if we know that he hear us, whatsoever we ask, we know that we have the petitions that we desired of him." - 1 John 5:15***

John says we know for certain he can hear us when we pray. Some have doubted for too long. It's because you've been disobedient or you haven't been in the word of God. Maybe you haven't loved someone the way you ought. Maybe you just haven't been telling people about Jesus, or maybe you've never been saved at all. One thing we know about God is this--he hears us when we pray. Bring it to the Lord.

[1] ***Oral Legends***

Chapter 17: The Importance Of Fellowship

"This then is the message which we have heard of him, and declare unto you, that God is light, and in him is no darkness at all." – 1 John 1:5

"Clovis Chappell, a minister from a century back, used to tell the story of two paddleboats. They left Memphis about the same time, traveling down the Mississippi River to New Orleans. As they traveled side by side, sailors from one vessel made a few remarks about the snail's pace of the other. Words were exchanged. Challenges were made. And the race began. Competition became vicious as the two boats roared through the Deep South. One boat began falling behind. Not enough fuel. There had been plenty of coal for the trip, but not enough for a race. As the boat dropped back, an enterprising young sailor took some of the ship's cargo and tossed it into the ovens. When the sailors saw that the supplies burned as well as the coal, they fueled their boat with the material they had been assigned to transport. They ended up winning the race, but burned their cargo in the process."[1]

I know that many who are reading this book are further along on their spiritual journey than others. If you are one of those believers who is a bit more mature in your faith, you may feel that this section of the book is beneath you. Yet, as I travel around the world and preach in churches of every sort, I find that in the midst of trying do the best that we can in life, succeed and even do God's will, we have sacrificed and burned up one of the greatest gifts we were ever given, and that is our fellowship with the family of God. What has happened to our fellowship with other believers? Have we forgotten that we are a family?

There is a lack of fellowship among couples today. Married couples have nothing more to say to each other after eight years according to a study. Professor Hans Jurgens asked 5000 German husbands and wives how often they talked to each other. After two years of marriage, most of them managed two or three minutes of chat over breakfast, more than twenty minutes over the evening meal and a few more minutes in bed. By the sixth year, that was down to ten minutes a day. A state of "almost total speechlessness" was reached by the eighth year of marriage. It's plain to see that there is a lack of fellowship among couples today.

There is a lack of fellowship among parents and their children today. A recent survey by America's most popular teen magazine revealed that only 4.1% of the teenage girls in America feel they could go to their father to talk about a serious problem. Even more recently, USA Today published the eye-opening results of a study of teens under stress. When asked where they turn for help in a crisis, the most popular choice was music, the second choice was peers, and the third was TV. Amazing as it may sound, moms were down the list at number thirty-one, and dads were forty- eighth. There is a lack of fellowship between Christian parents and their children.[1]

More than that, there is a lack of fellowship between Christians and their God. It was discovered by a study conducted by the Presbyterian Church that the average pastor in America today of any denomination prays less than three minutes a day. It is plain to see that there is a lack of fellowship between Christians and their God.

The reason that most Christians are not in fellowship with the family of God is because they don't realize that they aren't in fellowship with the family of God. Many reading this book are going to finish it as the same person they were when they first cracked the cover, because they won't realize that God is desperately trying to speak to them.

"That which was from the beginning, which we have heard, which we have seen with our eyes, which we have looked upon, and our hands have handled, of the Word of life; (For the life was manifested, and we have seen it, and bear witness, and shew unto you that eternal life, which was with the Father, and was manifested unto us;) That which we have seen and heard declare we unto you, that ye also may have fellowship with us: and truly our fellowship is with the Father, and with his Son Jesus Christ. And these things write we unto you, that your joy may be full."
- 1 John 1:1-4

You know what I like about John? He reminds me of my father when he talks. I think he'd probably remind you of a lot of your fathers as well. What is he saying here that reminds me of my dad? He says, "Listen, before we even get started, I just want you to know that everything I'm going to tell you is for your joy" (paraphrase mine). In other words, I'm telling you this for your own good. Now isn't that just like a daddy? What else does he say that sounds just like a father? He says, "I'm telling you all this because I've seen it, I've been there and I know what I'm talking about" (paraphrase mine), sounds just like my dad, "Son, I was doing this long before you were ever born. I think I know what I'm saying." And as much as that gets on our nerves growing up, our fathers always turned out to be right about it, didn't they?

In the same way, John's right about this. He says, "I'm telling you these things because I've seen them happen; I've walked with Jesus, I've seen men saved and I'm telling you all of these things so that you will be happier" (paraphrase mine). John ought to resemble a father; everything that he says in First John is about the family of God.

THERE IS NO FELLOWSHIP WITH GOD

"If we say that we have fellowship with him, and walk in darkness, we lie, and do not the truth:" – 1 John 1:6

Just like we said before, the great thing about John is that he gives us the facts. He tells us the things we can know for certain as simply as he can tell them. The thing he tells us here is this: if you're living in sin, if you're in darkness, then you cannot have fellowship with God. It does not matter how great or small the sin seems.

Blinding Lights

John describes it like this. God is in a bright place of light, so if the place in which you find yourself is dark, then you're obviously not in the same place as God. The ultimate blinding light is God himself.

I had a woman approach me at my first church whose husband had left her, yet she was still married to him. Claiming that God told her to go to a bar so that she could get her mind off things, she sounded so eloquent you would almost believe the filth she was saying. So she went to the bar, not to drink mind you, just to go dancing with people who were drunk. She sat there for a while, then she got up and danced with two or three men and by the end of the night her mind was definitely at ease. She said, "Brother Braxton, isn't God good? He brought me the best man in that bar that night to slow dance with. He just held me and I forgot all about my husband. God sure is great isn't he?"

I want to tell you, God is never going to command us to enter a place of sin except perhaps to tell men about him. God didn't send her there that night; it was the counterfeit, the devil. God didn't bring her some other man with whom she's not married. God didn't make that woman forget about her husband. Do you know where God would've had her--at her house praying for her husband to come home.

John's just a simple fisherman, but he can see the simple truth here. If Jesus walks in the light and you're walking in a place that is the least bit dark, then you are not walking with him, and you're not in fellowship with him. You had better make sure that every day of your life you are as sin-free as possible, because if you are not, then you're walking through this world all by yourself and this world is a scary place without God.

Making decisions in the dark can lead to some regrettable consequences. Back in the days before electricity, a tightfisted old farmer was taking his hired man to task for carrying a lighted lantern when he went to call on his best girl. "Why," he exclaimed, "When I went a-courtin' I never carried one of them things. I always went in the dark."

"Yes," the hired man said wryly," and look what you got!"

There is a simple truth in that story; you better not make choices in your life without being in fellowship with God, walking right beside him. If you do, then you're relying on your own instincts and those instincts are worldly. The Bible calls it worldly wisdom.

Consider the biggest mistakes you've made in your life. I don't mean sinful things; I just mean bad choices. You may have thought you were doing the right thing, but in the end it turned out bad for you. I don't know your situation, but I'll guarantee you that you made that choice during a moment in your life when you were in darkness and not walking side by side with God. I'll guarantee you that when that decision was made, you had some sin, great or small, in your life you hadn't dealt with.

Now, I don't know how to make this picture of our relationship with God any clearer to lady readers, but I know that the men understand completely and I'll tell you why. How many of you men, I wonder, have ever gone and tried to pick out a gift for your wife on your own with no help? I can pick out a blouse for her or a skirt or something and bring it home and she'll think it's the greatest thing in the world. I'm on a roll! I might go back and get her one that looks just exactly the same the next week and she wouldn't wear it if her life depended on it. I can't understand it. I don't see the difference, but she does. On the other hand, we can go to a store together and every dress looks the same to me, every skirt is the same, but she'll find the last one I'd have ever picked.

That's true for me now and it'll be true in thirty years, but sometimes we think that we've been Christians long enough and been in church long enough that we know what choices to make on our own. Listen, you don't really have a clue what God wants from you unless he's right there with you the whole time showing you. Strangely, the thing he often wants you to do, the place he wants you to go, and the job he has for you is the last one you would have ever picked for yourself. The steps of a righteous man are ordered of the Lord. We must be in the light as he is in the light.

There Is No Fellowship With Believers

"But if we walk in the light, as he is in the light, we have fellowship one with another, and the blood of Jesus Christ his Son cleanseth us from all sin." – 1 John 1: 7

Then John says, "If you walk in the light where Jesus is, you'll also be walking with other believers." Now that makes sense doesn't it? If Jesus is there and I'm walking with him and you're walking with him as well, then we're both walking with each other, aren't we?

You've got a treasure here that you're not taking advantage of. There are times when my wife was in school, but I needed someone to talk to, a shoulder to cry on and I knew that at church I had people like that. I knew of people who could cheer me up. Granted, the things they say to cheer me up aren't always the best choice of words.

I remember as a child coming home from school, feeling bad and telling my father, "Dad, nobody likes me," looking to him for some word of hope he would say back to me.

"Son, he answered, "Don't say that. Not everyone's met you yet." Despite the choice of words, he was trying to help me because he loves me and we're a family.

You know, there are a lot of believers that I don't have a thing in common with. There is no reason why we ought to be friends and there is no reason why we ought to have conversation except that we both have Jesus in common and that's enough. When you realize that you are the property of God, you realize that you've got God in common with every person and everything at church. We've got to be in fellowship with God's people because most of the time they're the only ones we can trust.

Two men were out hunting in the northern U.S. Suddenly, one yelled and the other looked up to see a grizzly charging them. The first started to frantically put on his tennis shoes, and his friend anxiously asked, "What are you doing? Don't you know you can't outrun a grizzly bear?"

"I don't have to outrun a grizzly. I just have to outrun you!" That is the mentality of the world today.[2]

Why should you, in this modern day, care to fellowship with the family of God? There is one simple reason and it's this; you can't trust the world. Fortunately, if we are all in the light as he is in the light, we know we have fellowship with one another. More than that, if we are all in the light as he is in the light, we'll all be heading in the same direction.

Do you know why churches split apart? It's not because of music or preaching. Churches split because God is speaking, and only half the people are hearing him. Have you ever felt God telling you to pray about something or moving you to do something, and then you find out that someone else felt the same way? That's because that in that moment, you and that person were both walking with God and he spoke something you both heard. Can you imagine what God's people could do if we would all walk with him and listen to him in unison every moment of every day of our lives?

THERE IS NO FELLOWSHIP WITH THE HOLY SPIRIT

"If we confess our sins, he is faithful and just to forgive us our sins, and to cleanse us from all unrighteousness." - 1 John 1:9

So, we know that we are not always in fellowship with God and that when we are not, it's because we are in sin. We know what could be accomplished if God's people would all walk daily with him, but how do we walk daily with him? It's an answer that we all know so well, but so few of us apply to our lives. Just confess.

1www.Sermonillustrations.com
2Source Unknown

Chapter 18: Knowing The Enemy

In this chapter, I want us to talk about one of the biggest threats to the family of God. Those of us who are saved know one thing with certainty about the enemy. The devil is going to attack you from every direction. One of the ways that he is going to try and destroy you is from within.

The devil, as many of you have already seen, will try and destroy you with some of the people in your life, people you trust the most. He'll try and destroy you with your wife. He'll try and destroy you with your husband. He'll try and destroy you with your parents, or he just might try and use you to destroy someone else. You might say, "But you're talking about Christian folks here." That's right; I am. But the devil will use you or the people around you to destroy God's work if you'll only let him.

Danger In The Family

"Little children, it is the last time: and as ye have heard that antichrist shall come, even now are there many antichrists; whereby we know that it is the last time. They went out from us, but they were not of us; for if they had been of us, they would no doubt have continued with us: but they went out, that they might be made manifest that they were not all of us." – 1 John 2:18-19

Now, what is John talking about here? Is he talking about the antichrist that we learn about in Revelation who's going to ride in on a white horse and deceive the world with peace? Well, not exactly. John refers to that antichrist, but there are some antichrists present right now. They're deceiving people the way that antichrist will, but they are doing it at present. Well, where are they? These antichrists are in the church.

John says there are antichrists around even now, and every now and then, one of them will poke his or her head out and start causing trouble with God's people, making them doubt God's men and meddling with the church. I believe I've met a few antichrists in my day, haven't you? John says they place doubt in people's minds about what they believe.

In 1887, the coffin of Abraham Lincoln was pried open to determine if it contained his body. What makes that act so remarkable is the fact that Lincoln's body had rested in that coffin for 22 years. Yet, even more amazing is that 14 years later a rumor circulated again that Lincoln's coffin was actually empty. The furor so gripped the land that the only way to silence it was to dig up the coffin-- again. This was done and the rumor silenced when a handful of witnesses viewed the lifeless body of Abraham Lincoln.[1]

Listen, there are antichrists out there who are placing doubt in people's minds about Christians and Christianity in places you'd never suspect. In Christian colleges, there are professors who take joy in knocking down the faith of a young passionate man or woman by showing them how the Bible might contradict itself and they say it's to strengthen the faith of such kids, but 20-year-old students, who were only moments before on fire for God, are now walking out of a room with tears in their eyes, doubting what they always believed. Jesus said anyone who would weaken the faith of a child of God would be better off having a millstone hanged about his neck and being cast into the sea. It's a serious thing when you start talking about making people doubt.

You'll do it and never realize you've done it. I don't know how many stories I've heard about someone who came to church and, while someone was singing, a couple of church members started criticizing her right there in their pew where they thought no one could hear, but someone did hear and decided that if that's the kind of backstabbers Christians are, they didn't want to be one. Who are these antichrists? That's anyone who leads someone else away from Jesus.

You'll run into a lot of antichrists who you never knew were antichrists. Listen, good godly family members who are saved will speak the words of an antichrist and you'll never know it. On that Sunday, when you feel like you just don't want to go to church, that saved person that you love will say, "Why don't you just stay home today?" That saved person, in a time when you are having financial trouble, will tell you, "Oh, you don't need to tithe that much this week, just wait." And, all the while, they think they're telling you a good thing. They think they're helping you, but they are delivering a message from the enemy. How many preachers have quite the ministry because their wife, another preacher or a friend said, "God will understand if you want to take a break for a while?"

There is a preacher I know very well who got depressed about the size of his church. He had been there forever. His wife loved him and got to feeling bad for him and said, "Honey you've been at this thing for years; why don't you just take a break," and so he did. She wanted him to go see a psychologist, and so he did. The psychologist that he went to see was a woman, and she came onto him, seduced him, committed adultery with him and then threatened to tell his wife if he didn't give her so much money. Turns out this woman and her husband did this all the time. It ruined this poor man's ministry and it broke his heart. He lost his church, all because he listened to his wife instead of God; and without knowing it she was giving him a message from the antichrist. The scary thing is that you'll find yourself delivering an antichristian message and not even realize it.

Defense For The Family

"But ye have an unction from the Holy One, and ye know all things. I have not written unto you because ye know not the truth, but because ye know it, and that no lie is of the truth." – 1 John 2: 20-21

What is John talking about when he says that we know all these things? Luke chapter 24:44-45 says:

"And he said unto them, These are the words which I spake unto you, while I was yet with you, that all things must be fulfilled,

which were written in the law of Moses, and in the prophets, and in the psalms, concerning me. Then opened he their understanding, that they might understand the scriptures,"
- Luke 24:44-45

Of all of the miracles that Jesus performed and of all of people that Jesus healed and of all of the death that Jesus stopped outside of the miracle of our salvation, this miracle is perhaps the greatest. Here we see that the last miracle that Jesus performs on earth is when he gives his followers the ability to understand the Bible. There are many things that I do not understand, but thanks to this verse, God's Word is not one of them. I do not understand why anybody enjoys cottage cheese, but God did not give me the ability to understand cottage cheese.

Some times I'll walk into a room and look at God's Word sitting there, and I know I ought to be reading it, but I've got something more pressing to do. You know what the convicting thought is that goes through my mind? There are people in other parts of the world, who would give anything to just get to sit down and read that thing in freedom, and soak up everything God's saying to them, but I walk past it day by day without a care.

Why does John tell us this? He says, "You who serve God know better than to follow these antichrists because you have an understanding of the Word of God. You don't have to fall into Satan's trap" (paraphrase mine). Since they might be family members, or they might be friends, you had better guard yourself the way that John says to guard yourself and that's by walking daily with God in prayer.

We are so blessed by the omnipresence of God, that no matter where we are or what we are doing we can simply speak and he hears. He is in the room with you right now. If I'm sitting in my office, and a friend walks in and sits down, I speak to him, but imagine what it would be like if I simply stood up and walked out of the room without ever acknowledging my friend's presence. Common courtesy tells you not to do that, but how many times do we wake up in the morning and walk right past Jesus without a word? We eat our breakfast and walk passed him out the door never saying a word. We drive to work and Jesus is in the car, but we get out and shut the door without ever saying a word. We go home at night without ever saying a word, but all the while, Jesus is there waiting to speak to us and waiting for us to speak to him. He's got things that he wants to tell you. There are things you need to tell him--if only to tell him that you love him.

Sadly, the simple common courtesy that we extend to all our other friends we can't extend to Jesus, and though he's standing face to face with us as a friend all day long, we walk on by without a word. So, guard yourself from the traps of the enemy, because these antichrists are hidden where you would never expect them to be.

DENIAL OF THE FAMILY

"Who is a liar but he that denieth that Jesus is the Christ? He is antichrist, that denieth the Father and the Son. Whosoever denieth the Son, the same hath not the Father: he that acknowledgeth the Son hath the Father also. Let that therefore abide in you, which ye have heard from the beginning. If that which ye have heard from the beginning shall remain in you, ye also shall continue in the Son, and in the Father. And this is the promise that he hath promised us, even eternal life. These things have I written unto you concerning them that seduce you. But the anointing which ye have received of him abideth in you, and ye need not that any man teach you: but as the same anointing teacheth you of all things, and is truth, and is no lie, and even as it hath taught you, ye shall abide in him. And now, little children, abide in him; that, when he shall appear, we may have confidence, and not be ashamed before him at his coming. If ye know that he is righteous, ye

know that every one that doeth righteousness is born of him. *– 1 John 2:22-29*

John closes by taking away our excuses. He says, "If he abides in you, you can have confidence. You can be sure and you don't have to be ashamed when he comes back one day." (paraphrase mine).

So, we have no excuse if we deny Christ. How do we deny Christ? We deny Christ when we listen to others instead of him--such as those antichrists. We deny Christ when we become one of those antichrists to someone else, but remember, you who are Christians have no excuse to ever fall victim to the deception of these people because you have a power, a power to understand God's Word. You can see with spiritual eyes.

[1] ***Oral Legend***

Chapter 19: Becoming A Blinding Light

"Behold, what manner of love the Father hath bestowed upon us, that we should be called the sons of God: therefore the world knoweth us not, because it knew him not."
- 1 John 3:1

How many of you have ever been told that you look like one of your parents? Oh, every one of us has either got our mother's nose or our father's eyes or our uncle's ears. Some of you would trade every bit of that for their hair, wouldn't you?

I want you to know that the same is true of your relationship to your spiritual Father. The wonderful truth of the Bible is that we aren't just going to have parts and pieces that look like Jesus, if we've truly been saved, we will look so much like Christ that the world will not be able to tell the difference.

If you are in the family of God, you ought to somewhat resemble him. There is a lot of talk about who God is in the world today. Some people in the Christian community say that God is a woman, and I do not believe that. Some people say that God is a man, but that does not do him justice. Some people say that he is a genderless being, but that does not explain to me what God really is. Of all of the labels we could place on him, of all of the names we could give him, of all of the positions we could assign to him, the one that means the most to me that I can cling to is Father. He's Father.

If he's my Father, I am going to look something like him. There are going to be traits that are present in him that ought to be present in me. Now, you may not want to look like your earthly father, but you ought to want to look like your Heavenly Father. John is going to give us some clues as to what Jesus is going to look like. And as he does, I want you to ask yourself, "If I saw Jesus standing next to me in some spiritual way, how much would I look like him?"

We once had a church yard sale when I was pastoring, and I observed something that I will never forget. A little boy's mother had decided to sell his GI Joes. She thought it was time for him to give up the things of childhood. In case you ever need to know this, the way to keep your GI Joes is to write your name on their legs. Who wants a

GI Joe with someone else's name on it? Frustrated at the thought of being separated from his plastic friends, this boy had done just that. Standing by, I watched as an elderly woman with a rag wiped the child's name off of each action figure. However, not to be daunted, the boy followed behind at a safe distance writing his name again on each of his toys.

The Christian life is not so different. Every day the devil is working on us, confusing us and trying to get us to remove those things from our lives that make us uniquely Christian, and God is waiting all along to fix us back the way we are supposed to be. As we study this, I pray that you will allow God to show you the things in your life that make you uniquely Christian, things that the Devil has removed, and let God freely work to restore them.

Clothes Of Christ

"Behold, what manner of love the Father hath bestowed upon us, that we should be called the sons of God: therefore the world knoweth us not, because it knew him not. Beloved, now are we the sons of God, and it doth not yet appear what we shall be: but we know that, when he shall appear, we shall be like him; for we shall see him as he is. And every man that hath this hope in him

purifieth himself, even as he is pure."– 1 John 3:1-3

Now, the thing about this scripture that we've just read is that it says that we really don't know what Jesus is going to look like; we just know that we're going to look like him when he comes. You might say, "That's silly! I know what Jesus is going to look like. We've got a picture at church; I've seen it." Well, maybe that's what he looks like and maybe it's not, but John says we really don't know what he's going to look like. But, even though we don't know what he's going to look like, we know that were going to look like him.

I am a huge fan of the Andy Griffith Show. I believe that Barney Fife is one of the greatest characters ever created by the entertainment world. And the more I watch of Barney Fife, the more I start thinking he's exactly what Christians ought to be. I know that sounds strange, but he fits the description that John gives here of what we as Christians are. John says that we ought to try to be the way Jesus is going to be even though we don't really know what he looks like. That's Barney. He doesn't have a clue what a real sheriff's deputy is supposed to be like. He's got some crazy ideas about the matter, but he really doesn't know. Yet, even though he has no clue what a deputy ought to be like, he tries his hardest to be a good deputy.

He wears the uniform that a deputy ought to wear and carries a gun, even if Andy makes him keep the bullets in his pocket. I remember one time they were doing evaluations of the state's police officers, and one of the requirements was that you had to weigh over 140 pounds. Barney wanted so badly to be what a deputy ought to be that he wore a heavy chain around his neck and hid it underneath his shirt so that he could pass. Just like a Christian, he always fouls things up, he always does the wrong thing and Andy always has to come and fix the things that he's done.

I want to tell you if we're doing what we ought to be doing as Christians, we're going to be a lot like Barney. John says we don't really know what Jesus is going to look like, but we know that when he comes back, we're going to look like him. I'll tell you now that the best thing that you can do is be a Christian Barney Fife. Get up every morning and to the best of your ability put on the Christian uniform which Paul calls the armor of God. Get that one bullet that you keep in your pocket (the Word of God) and fight the Christian fight, knowing that if somewhere along the way you stumble and foul things up, you can always rely on Jesus, not Andy, to come along and fix the things that you've done wrong.

If you stand Barney next to Andy, Barney's going to look pretty puny. He's not going to have the muscles Andy's got to fill out that shirt. He's not going to have that jaw line that the ladies love. He's not always going to have the right thing to say in hard times, but the one thing that's true about him is that he's wearing the uniform and he's carrying the tools.

I want to ask you a question, "If you were placed next to Jesus, what would you look like?" I'll guarantee you that you are not going to have all the wonderful attributes that make you exactly like Jesus until the day you arrive in heaven and are then glorified. Perhaps all you are is a faint resemblance of Jesus, but if you're wearing the uniform (the clothes of a Christian) and your arming yourself daily with the Word of God, then you've done what John requires. The problem arises when we want to remove that uniform.

Every year we used to go to Gatlinburg, Tennessee. When I was growing up, I remember very clearly several things that happened on those trips. You may have been to this place, but there is a haunted house off on a side street in Gatlinburg, and every year I would beg my daddy to take me there. Every year the same thing happened, my older brother would taunt me and say, "You're too much of a coward, you're too much of a scaredy cat, you're too wimpy to go through that haunted house."

Well, that encouraged me even more. We would get out there every time, just me and my father, and we would prepare to go through that haunted house. As we would stand before the doorway, my father would say, "Are you sure you want to do this?"

I would say, "Daddy, I'm not a coward, I'm not a scaredy cat and I'm not a wimp. I want to go through."

We would always go in the door and pay our five dollars. As we would walk into that first room of the haunted house, there was a bat painted on the wall. It wasn't even real, and every year when I would see that bat, I would stop in my tracks, stare at it for a couple of seconds and then let out the most blood-curdling scream. My father would always get his money back and we would leave.

I'll never forget the last time that it ever happened. As we were walking down the sidewalk going back to the hotel, just my father and I, I said, "Daddy?"

"Yes son?"

"I'm a coward, aren't I?"

He would say, "Yes, son, you're a coward."

"I'm a scaredy cat, too."

"Yes, son, you're a scaredy cat."

"I'm a wimp, aren't I, daddy?"

"Yes, son, you're a wimp."

Then I said, "Well, daddy, I don't mind being a coward, a scaredy cat and a wimp just as long as you'll promise me one thing."

He said, "What's that?"

I said, "Just don't let anyone else find out."

In the Christian life many times, that's how we are. We want to do the right thing; we set our goal to do the right thing, but the first time the devil tempts us or rears his ugly head, we will abandon the commitments, resolutions, goals and promises that we have committed to the Almighty and turn wholeheartedly running in the other direction, leaving Jesus behind because we are cowardly scardy cats and wimpy Christians.

Listen, I'll be honest with you. I think some of you are like me. I'm never embarrassed to wear the clothes of a Christian. I'm not embarrassed to be one, but the way other Christians act, I'm embarrassed to be grouped with them. We ought to be out there in full Christian garb every chance we get so that the world sees the real Christ in us, even if it's a puny little Barney Fife version of Jesus. It would be better if they saw that then what other Christians might bring them.

CLEAN AS CHRIST

"Whosoever committeth sin transgresseth also the law: for sin is the transgression of

the law. And ye know that he was manifested to take away our sins; and in him is no sin. Whosoever abideth in him sinneth not: whosoever sinneth hath not seen him, neither known him. Little children, let no man deceive you: he that doeth righteousness is righteous, even as he is righteous. He that committeth sin is of the devil; for the devil sinneth from the beginning. For this purpose the Son of God was manifested, that he might destroy the works of the devil. Whosoever is born of God doth not commit sin; for his seed remaineth in him: and he cannot sin, because he is born of God. In this the children of God are manifest, and the children of the devil: whosoever doeth not righteousness is not of God, neither he that loveth not his brother."– 1 John 3:4-10

It sure looks like the above verse says that if you sin at all, even once, you're not saved. The thing you've got to remember is that it says, "commit sin." Verse eight says he that "committeth sin." It never says, "He that commits a sin." It says, "committeth sin" or "commit sin." That word is progressive; it means if you go on sinning again and again and the Holy Spirit doesn't trouble you about it, then you must not be saved, because there is no evidence of the Holy Spirit in your life. You see, the matter of importance is not so much the sin that is present in your life; instead, it's how you handle that sin.

In 1884, Grover Cleveland was running against James G. Blaine for the presidency of the U.S. Blaine supporters discovered that Cleveland, who was a bachelor at the time, had fathered a son by Mrs. Maria Crofts Halpin, an attractive widow who had been on friendly terms with several politicians. Subsequently, republicans tried to pin an immorality tag on democrat Cleveland by distributing handbills showing an infant labeled, "One more vote for Cleveland," and by having paraders chant, "Ma, Ma, where's my pa? Gone to the White House, Ha, Ha, Ha!" The move, however, backfired badly. Rather than deny the story, Cleveland decided to tell the truth and admit the intimacy. This candor helped defuse the issue, and Cleveland was elected president. It's all about confession.[1]

A saved man, when he realizes he's sinned, will get on his knees and ask God to forgive him. From that point on, he'll try his best not to commit that sin again. The way that Jimmy Swaggart handled his sin was the right way. After committing sexual acts with prostitutes, he got on his knees and asked God to forgive him first, and second, he stood before the church and confessed.

There is a church in Madison, Tennessee, called Cornerstone that has done more to promote the cause of Christ in the Nashville area than many others. Their pastor is a convicted murderer, but he got on his knees, gave it to God and changed his life.

The fact of the matter is that Jimmy Swaggart's sin may be a thousand times worse than any sin you ever committed, but if you didn't get on your knees the minute you realized you hade done wrong, then you haven't handled your sin in as Christian a way as Jimmy Swaggart did.

How many times was poor old Barney left there in the jail house to watch over some criminals that were locked up? Somehow those criminals convinced old Barney to unlock the door, and they always escaped. What does Barney do? He doesn't try to hide it because he knows there is no way he can. He doesn't try to keep it a secret. As much as he hates to, he goes to Andy with shame on his face and his tail between his legs and confesses, "Andy, something awful happened."

John doesn't say that Christians won't commit a sin; he says they won't go on in sin, and some of the greatest memories I have of my Christian walk are the times when I went to God with shame on my face and my tail between my legs and said, "God, I don't won't to tell you, but I've done something awful." He forgives me and I'm clean. Christians won't live a life of sin because the righteous man and the righteous woman will get on their knees the moment they commit a sin and get it out of their lives.

The Prussian king, Frederick the Great, was once touring a Berlin prison. The prisoners fell on their knees before him to proclaim their innocence -- except for one man, who remained silent. Frederick called to him, "Why are you here?"

"Armed robbery, Your Majesty," was the reply.

"And are you guilty?"

"Yes indeed, Your Majesty. I deserve my punishment."

Frederick then summoned the jailer and ordered him, "Release this guilty wretch at once. I will not have him kept in this prison where he will corrupt all the fine innocent people who occupy it."[2]

How do we know if someone else is a blinding light? John says:

> *"If ye know that he is righteous, ye know that every one that doeth righteousness is born of him." -1 John 2:29*

CARE OF CHRIST

Based on these things it becomes clear that if a person wants to become like Christ and thus a glaring evidence of the Christian faith, they must be caring as Christ is caring toward others. This is undeniable and cannot be missed. The greatest commandment is to love.

[1] *www.Sermonillustrations.com*
[2] *www.sermoncentral.com*

Chapter 20: True Love

"In this the children of God are manifest, and the children of the devil: whosoever doeth not righteousness is not of God, neither he that loveth not his brother. For this is the message that ye heard from the beginning, that we should love one another. Not as Cain, who was of that wicked one, and slew his brother. And wherefore slew he him? Because his own works were evil, and his brother's righteous. Marvel not, my brethren, if the world hate you. We know that we have passed from death unto life, because we love the brethren. He that loveth not his brother abideth in death. Whosoever hateth his brother is a murderer: and ye know that no murderer hath eternal life abiding in him. Hereby perceive we the love of God, because he laid down his life for us: and we ought to lay down our lives for the brethren." - 1 John 3:10-16

John says you ought to love your brother. Jesus laid down his life for you and you ought to be willing to lay your life down for someone else. It troubled me to hear just yesterday about someone who used a very profane and vulgar word in reference to someone else in our church. Sometimes our anger gets the better of us. The truth is, it doesn't matter if you like someone, if they're saved, they're your family. Jonah had to overcome this and love the people of Nineveh despite the history of hatred they had for the Hebrews.

I remember when I was a child that during the course of the year, I'd get mad at everyone in my family. I'd get mad at my mother, I'd get mad at my father and I'd get mad at my brother; but at Christmas time, I realized that I really did love them as we sat around the fireplace together.

In my first pastoral position, a young man came to our church and he said, "My mother is in the hospital; she's going to have surgery tomorrow and she may die. If she dies, I know she's lost and she'll go to hell. You've got to talk to her."

I walked into her hospital room, took her by the hand and we talked about life. I said to her, "Ma'am, do you know for sure that if you died today you would go to Heaven?"

She said, "Oh, no sir, I live a life as filthy as anyone in this town. The Lord wouldn't let me into Heaven."

I said, "If you'll just confess that to God today, you can be saved." She opened her mouth very weakly and began to pray as best she could. She began to confess things to God that I would have never dreamed and, in the end, she prayed for Christ to come into her life and make her new. When she was finished, she looked over at me and she was crying like a baby. I said, "Why are you crying?"

She said, "I never new how good it would feel to confess; I feel clean."

She looked at me and said, "You're crying, too."

I looked on the other side of the room and her daughter was crying. I turned around and the nurse was crying. We all cried together as she got right with God. She lost the use of her legs, but she wanted to be baptized. So, we got some men to pick up her wheelchair and lower her down into that baptistery. She got baptized and served the Lord faithfully for as long as I was at that church.

"Beloved, let us love one another: for love is of God; and every one that loveth is born of God, and knoweth God. He that loveth not knoweth not God; for God is love." - 1 John 4:7,8

Why do you love Jesus? There are a lot of good reasons to serve Jesus but there are also a lot of bad ones. It is very possible to serve Jesus without ever really loving him. Why Jesus?

There are a lot of good reasons for a man to marry a woman, but there are a lot of bad reasons. A lot of men marry a particular woman because they know that if they marry her, they get to have her body, but that's not a good reason to marry her. Many men marry that particular woman because they know that she would make a good wife and mother. Once again, that's not a good reason to marry her. Some men marry a particular woman because she's going to look good by his side, but that's not a good reason to marry her either.

The truth is that a lot of Christians love Jesus because he died on the cross for them. That's not why the Bible says you ought to love him. A lot of Christians love Jesus because he saved them from a devil's hell, but that's not why the Bible says you ought to love Jesus. A lot of Christians love Jesus because he's made their lives so wonderful and blessed them so, but that's not why the Bible says you ought to love Jesus. Why ought you to love him? In this chapter, I want us to see what the love between you and Jesus ought to be.

Look at the verse again. God is love. Now, we've seen that if we are going to look like him, we know that we've got to be righteous. In the last chapter, we saw that we don't know what we shall be, but we know that when Jesus comes, if there is one thing that we can know for sure, it's that he'll be righteous. So if we can dress ourselves in righteousness, we will look like him. So, we find that God is love, and there are several things that are going to happen to us when we come to understand the love of God.

God Loved Us, So We Love Each Other

"Beloved, if God so loved us, we ought also to love one another."– 1 John 4:11

You might say about someone, "I don't want to be in a family with them. I don't like them." A lot of you know some Christians who you just don't like. Your job is not to like them; your job is to love them. There are inevitably going to be people you don't like. Did Jesus like everyone? He loved everyone, but he didn't like everyone. What about the Pharisees that followed Jesus around, pointed fingers at him and waiting for him to make a mistake? Did he like them? What did he call them? He called them whited sepulchers, full of dead men's bones. It doesn't sound too complimentary, does it? What if I said to my wife on Valentines Day, "Hey there, my little whited sepulcher full of dead men's bones?" There were some people Jesus didn't like. You don't have to like everyone, but you do have to love everyone.

I hated our dog when we first got her. I hated her. She went potty on everything. She had to go outside every five minutes. She chewed on things, jumped on you at the wrong time and just made life miserable. There was nothing about that animal that I liked, but Sarah loved her. I didn't understand it. I probably still wouldn't understand it except for one thing. When that dog was annoying me, barking and doing everything I hate, Sarah would say, "Isn't she cute? Isn't she cute when she does that? Isn't she cute when she rolls around like that? Isn't she pretty? Isn't she funny?" At first I could not see anything cute about a dog going potty on the carpet. It took me a long time. But, finally, after months of Sarah pointing out the good things and never the bad, I started to like the mongrel dog a little bit. A few more weeks and I really liked her. Finally, I learned to love that little mutt. I'm talking about an animal. Now, maybe that's because somewhere along the way she got potty trained, but the argument still works.

When you realize that God is love, it changes you the same way. Do you love Jesus? Would you like to know how to love any Christian? If they're a Christian, guess who lives inside of them. Love the Jesus in them and you'll find yourself loving that Christian too. Your love may not be enough to connect you to that person, but God"s love is. Karl Barth, a famed theologian, was once asked, "What is the greatest thought you have ever had?" And he said, "Jesus loves me this I know for the Bible tells me so." Don't pretend to love someone. Instead, look beyond your differences and find the Jesus in one another, and if your love for him is sincere, your love for them can be too.

John says, "The way I see it, if you love Jesus and that person you don't like has got Jesus inside of him, then you ought to love him for the Jesus that's there" (paraphrase mine).

We've got a picture at our house of Sarah and me that I hate. Now, the fact of the matter is, I don't take bad pictures, but in this one, I have a really goofy look on my face, but Sarah looks great in it. You know what, it's the worst picture of me that exists, but it's one of my favorites because of the way Sarah looks in it, and that's why I leave it displayed at the house.

John says that if you'll look for the Jesus inside of them, and you'll work on loving the Jesus inside of them, you'll end up loving that person whether you meant to or not. That's a wonderful thing that happens to you when you learn that God is love and what it means to be in love with God, but the question of why you ought to love Jesus has still not been answered.

God Loved Us, So We Have No Fear

"There is no fear in love; but perfect love casteth out fear: because fear hath torment. He that feareth is not made perfect in love."
– 1 John 4:18

Now John is saying that if you really love God and you know that he loves you, you ought never to fear, because you know that he'll never leave you.

I've been a youth minister twice, and there is one thing that I have noticed about teenagers today that has already changed since I was a teenager five years ago. When they find someone they like, they make it so complicated. Do you know what I mean? I believe it's probably because so many of them have parents who've been divorced and they don't want the same thing to happen to them. They are afraid. Well, if you really are in love, you don't ever have to be afraid of that. Still, these teenagers are afraid and it alters the way they act. They analyze everything about their relationship, don't they? "Well, why do I love him?" Or, "How do I know I love her?" Everything that one of them says is put under a microscope by the other. "What did he mean by that?" Some poor guy says that he likes the girl's skirt, and you know what happens. She gets upset because she wants to know why he didn't compliment her blouse. And the poor girl, if she even mentions a boy that she used to date, her new boyfriend all of a sudden gets jealous. It's just gotten so complex.

When I laid eyes on Sarah, I didn't ask myself why I felt the way I did. I didn't talk to a school psychologist about how I knew for sure if I loved her or not. I just said "Whooo! I want to be with her!" Moreover, when I found out that she loved me and I knew for sure that I loved her, I asked God if we could be together and I didn't have a thing to fear because love casts out all fears, according to John.

Unfortunately, human beings can't give perfect love. It doesn't matter how much a husband and wife love each other, they're still probably going to have World War III in their house at times. It doesn't matter how much you parents love your children, you don't have perfect love for them. I'll guarantee you they're going to do something every now and then that will make you want to wring their neck. On a human level, you can't give perfect love. Perfect love has got to come from God. But if you've got the Holy Spirit inside of you, then you can let the love of God show through him onto the world.

Perfect love casts out fear. And just like I don't ever have to worry about Sarah leaving me because of the confidence I have in our love, I don't have to fear God ever leaving me, because I know that as strong as the love in my marriage might be, God gives me a stronger love, a perfect love.

These truths are never more important than for those who have been in the midst of a broken relationship. If there was ever anyone who needed to hear about perfect love, it's them. Perhaps you have been through a divorce and have been so damaged by that event that you fear ever involving yourself in a relationship again. Perfect love casts out fear. So much power exists in that statement. Love creates confidence. Yet, our questions about love have not been thoroughly answered.

These are all wonderful things that happen to a person when he learns that God is love and what it means to be in love with God, but that still doesn't tell us why the Bible says we ought to love Jesus

God Loved Us, So We Love Him

"We love him, because he first loved us."
– 1 John 4: 19

What is the one good reason for loving God? It's because he first loved us.

If a man marries a woman because he wants her body, it doesn't matter how beautiful she is, one day his desire for her will fade. Similarly, if a man loves

God because of what was done for him at Calvary, his gratitude will fade.

What's the one thing that will keep a man in love with his wife? He's got to love her just because she loves him. If it's anything else, that relationship will not last. The same is true of your love for Jesus Christ. Why do you love him? Why Jesus?

Let me ask you a question that I think will put this in perspective for you. If you knew that there was no danger of hell, no hope of heaven, no reward and no punishment, no reason to love Jesus other than just because God told you to and he brought you together, would you love him anyway?

Chapter 21: Three Tools For The Journey

"Who is he that overcometh the world, but he that believeth that Jesus is the Son of God?" - 1 John 5:5

Have you ever attempted to go on a diet? If so, then you know just what giving up sin is like. It seems that every time I try to go on a diet, either my wife or my mother decides they're going to make cookies. I walk in, smell those things and I am no longer in control of my body. Trying to hold on, I go about my business; yet, because I smelled those cookies, I feel an emptiness inside. My stomach has done the work for me of clearing out some room. It has left memos all over the place to remind me of those cookies, and by the time I see them again, I have developed such a feeling of emptiness and such a desire that I fall face first into that plate of cookies and just don't care what it means any more.

Has that ever happened to you?

When I have tried to give things up for God in the past, I have felt that same emptiness. Strangely, that emptiness is often accompanied by loneliness. The result is a desire to fill that void. Just like your stomach, the devil will begin reminding you that there is room in your life for that sin. He will try and convince you that that sin will fill that void, and the question will become, "Is there anything keeping you from running to a plate full of sin?"

According to the scripture under discussion, all you have got to do to stay out of sin and overcome the world is believe in Jesus, right? Is that really all it takes? Well, yes and no. Believing in Jesus is all it takes to overcome the world, but the reason believing in Jesus is all it takes is this-- if you're really believing in Jesus, you're going to do what you ought to do to overcome the world. What if the coach of the Florida Gators told them, "All you've got to do to overcome that other team and win this game is just believe in yourself?"

Imagine if those guys did just that, walked out onto the field, stood there with their arms folded and said, "Well, I'm doing what the coach said. I believe that I could do this so I'm going to stand here believing. I mean that's all it takes." What's going to happen to them when the play starts? They'd all get their necks broken. They know better.

If the coach says, "Now, go out there and believe in yourself." Those players are going to go out there and win the game because, though all it takes is believing in themselves, if they really believe, they'll do what they know is necessary to win.

Is it just believing in Jesus that will allow us to overcome the sinful world? Yes, that's all it takes, and if we really believe, it takes more than standing around with our hands in our pockets, like so many Christians, waiting on heaven. Belief motivates behavior.

The Spirit

"This is he that came by water and blood, even Jesus Christ; not by water only, but by water and blood. And it is the Spirit that beareth witness, because the Spirit is truth. For there are three that bear record in heaven, the Father, the Word, and the Holy Ghost: and these three are one. And there are three that bear witness in earth, the Spirit, and the water, and the blood: and these three agree in one." – 1 John 5:6,7,8

Now, the first thing that the Bible says that you've got to have if you are going to overcome sin and stay out of that sin is the Spirit. Well, what is the Spirit? The Holy Spirit is the manifestation of

God that lives in the life of the believer. He comforts us, convicts us of sin and carries our prayers to the throne of God in heaven. The reason that preachers fall into sexual sin, parents beat their children and we fall short of perfection daily in our lives is because we don't have a close enough relationship to the Holy Spirit. You cannot avoid sin in your life without the Holy Spirit as your spiritual eye to see the sin of the world. You've heard that name Holy Spirit tossed around, but you've just written it off as a church word and never made it a serious part of your life. You won't survive without the Holy Spirit.

Imagine a father has a beautiful baby boy. There are a lot of reasons that a man might want to have a son. The man is going to have to change that baby's diaper and give that baby baths and talk to that baby in baby talk. Do you know why the man will do those things? Oh sure, he'll do it because of his love for the baby, but more than that, whether he knows it or not, one day he is going to grow old enough that he'll need someone to change his diaper and give him baths and talk baby talk to him. And that's what children are for. My brother, Chad, and I used to tell my parents, "We love you so much that we're going to keep you in the best nursing home ever." We'd ride down the road sitting in the back seat saying, "I think that one looks pretty good; what do you think? No, it's too fancy." But, putting all that aside, a man has got to change his baby's diaper and give the baby baths, and he's got to decide what kind of food the baby needs because the baby can't choose for himself. And everywhere that baby goes, mommy or daddy has got to be right there.

We can't do anything without the Holy Spirit. We are like a baby. We need that Holy Spirit there to communicate to us God's will for our lives. We could not even pick out our own food without him.

Do you know what life would be like without the Holy Spirit? You would not be able to pray to God on your own without the Holy Spirit. You would not be able to recognize sin without the Holy Spirit. You would not understand the Bible without the Holy Spirit. You would never have the ability to lead anyone to Jesus without the Holy Spirit and, finally, you could not go to heaven without the Holy Spirit. Jesus died on the cross in part to deliver the Holy Spirit into your heart. Jesus tore the veil so that you would no longer have to confess your sins to another person for forgiveness or guidance, but so that you could speak to him face to face through the Holy Spirit. I don't know if you've ever thought about it this way, but Christianity would not work without the Holy Spirit. Forgive me for the way this sounds, but most people don't understand how he works. It's the simplest thing in the world.

Blinding Lights

In the ninth grade, I was in the hospital for surgery on my hand. I still have the scar to this day. The bone inside of my hand snapped right in two and they had to operate to screw the bones back together. While I was in the recovery room, I met the most cold- hearted and ruthless woman you've ever seen. She was my nurse, and while I was lying there feeling half dead because of the anesthesia, she was slapping me in the face trying to wake me up. You know how it is when you're sleeping very well and someone starts bugging you. It's ten thousand times worse when you've been put to sleep with drugs. So, I determined somehow I was going to get even with her. When I finally came around and was pretty well awake, I realized that there was a button on my TV remote that sounded just like the "beep" on the monitoring machine attached to my body. I've seen enough hospitals on TV that I know if things beep too much it's bad. So I started "beeping" that thing. I started out slow and then I got that thing going like crazy. Sure enough, she came into my room, and so did everyone else looking terrified and scared to death that I was somehow in there dying.

Why did they all come running in there? It was because they knew that all of that racket meant something was going wrong. I want to remind you of something that I've had to tell myself lately. When you are about to encounter sin and you are about to step into one of Satan's attacks, the Holy Spirit will start beeping and chirping and making all kinds of racket to show you that something's not right and something's got to be changed. He warns us of sin and danger.

Unfortunately, those beeps get muffled after a while. We get to the point that we've heard them so long that we don't even notice them anymore. We used to live by the airport and I couldn't sleep at night for the planes flying overhead, but after a few years, I tried to hear them and I couldn't because I'd gotten so used to it. I'm glad for those who have cleaned up their lives and gotten the sin out, but if you're going to keep it out, then you've got to get back to the place where you hear the Holy Spirit's warning of sin. He makes just as much racket when you're about to lie as he would if you were about to kill someone.

Have you ever had a fight with your husband or wife? It just shows that one of you wasn't listening to the Holy Spirit, because if you were, he would have settled it. Have you ever taken a job and found out later it was the wrong job to take? If you'd been listening to the Holy Spirit, he wouldn't have let you take it. Have you ever dated someone who you shouldn't have? The list goes on. Every bad decision we've ever made is a result of ignoring the warning, the beeping, the chirping and the racket of the Holy Spirit.

Listening to him is the easiest thing you'll ever do because you don't have to do a thing; he does it for you.

THE WATER

"And there are three that bear witness in earth, the Spirit, and the water, and the blood: and these three agree in one." – 1 John 5:8

So, the number one thing that God gives us in order for us to overcome the world and the sin of the world is the Holy Spirit. Then, John says there is something else. He says there is water. Now, what does that water mean? Remember this, whenever we explore the Bible, if you find water mentioned going inside a person, that represents the Holy Spirit, However, if it's mentioned on the outside of someone, that is the Word of God. What does that word water mean here? ***"Husbands, love your wives, even as Christ also loved the church, and gave himself for it; That he might sanctify and cleanse it with the washing of water by the word," - Ephesians 5: 25,26*** This water we find here is the Word of God.

I look at sweet little ladies in churches today and I see women without sin. I believe with all of my heart that I could probably follow some elderly women around all day long and never find a sin that they have committed. Still, as sweet as these women might be, it is highly likely that while people like them may never go out and do something to voluntarily disobey God, they will sin in another way. There is the sin of commission and then there is the sin of omission. Sins of omission are things that God has commanded that you do but you don't do them, and therefore you fall into sin. In other words, you may not be out there telling someone to follow Mohammad, but you're not out there telling people about Jesus either. It is my personal opinion that the most common sin of omission that Christians commit is not studying their Bible like they should.

Now, let's put all of this aside and look at things logically. If we are going to overcome the world, the key is the Holy Spirit. The Holy Spirit helps you to overcome sin in a heart way (He speaks to your heart), but God also gives us a practical method for avoiding sin, and that's the Bible. In other words, the Holy Spirit says, "That's a sin, you ought to stay away from it," but it is your job to open the Bible and find out how to stay away from it in a practical way. Does that make sense to you?

Now, some of you who are having trouble knowing what you ought to be studying in your quiet time ought to look at what sins you are facing. Get a Bible with a good concordance and find where the Bible talks about them so you'll know what to do when you are faced with temptation. Cleanse yourself with the living water, the Bible.

Why do you think it was that the same John who wrote this letter was so touched when he saw that soldier pierce the body of Jesus? Out of Jesus' side came blood and *water*? That's right, water. It's because he saw a man who was so filled with the word and truth of God that when that body was pierced at death, the very thing that came pouring out of his lifeless body was the very thing that had poured out of his living body and that was the water, the Word of God.

Do you know what the two most unreliable creations on planet earth are? Undoubtedly, they are computers and cell telephones. Still, the wonderful thing about computers is that you can plug them up and just take the information from one and put it into the other. Now, why didn't God create us like that? Is the mind of a computer more powerful than the mind of a human being? No! The Bible is a holy book. Inside of it is all of the information you will ever need to live an exciting, fulfilling and pure life. All it takes is plugging it in and keeping it plugged in.

On one occasion I visited two different churches on the same day. In the morning, I visited a church in downtown Nashville. The people were wealthy, the music was exquisite, the preaching was eloquent and the service was orderly. However, nothing happened. There was no passion, nor was there excitement. No one seemed to be discussing the service as they left and, most people were watching the time from the first hymn. That evening I visited a country church with bluegrass music, middleclass congregants, moderate facilities, decent preaching and uncomfortable pews. Yet, people were engaged in the message, the altar was filled with teary-eyed sinners and everyone was discussing the message and the lives that were changed.

What happened at those two churches? Did God show up at that little country church just because he liked it more? Was that morning service so dry because God had slept in? No. Everyone at both churches was sitting in the presence of God. Congregants in both of those services were hearing the spoken Word of God as it was preached. Most individuals in both of those services had the Bible in their laps. The difference was that those who were at that little church way out in the middle of the country took the book that was sitting in their laps and plugged it into their lives. Believe it or not, it is an exciting feeling when all of a sudden you become enthusiastic about the Bible. It is the companion to the Holy Spirit's presence if you are to live the Christian life.

THE BLOOD

The Spirit is, of course, the Holy Spirit while the water is the Word and the blood is, of course, salvation.

Have you ever wondered why Jesus needed to die on the cross? According to the Old Testament, the way a Hebrew was cleansed of his sins was fairly complicated. At an appointed time, he would travel to the temple of God bringing with him the most pure sacrificial animal he had (in many cases a lamb, depending on the type of sacrifice). If he didn't have an unblemished animal, he could purchase one from vendors just outside of the temple. Either way, giving up that creature was a great sacrifice on the part of the Israelite man. When the priest spilt the blood of that animal, a great deal of blood was shed. The blood was the payment for whatever sin was in the life of the man.

Blood sacrifices in the Old Testament covered a man's sins, but not completely. By this I mean that his sins for a certain period of time were forgiven. Yet, when he left the temple that day and likely sinned before the setting of the sun, he already had need of a new sacrifice. Thus, in order to forgive the sins of a whole world of people, not just for an allotted time but all eternity, a perfect lamb needed to be slain, and the eternal blood of an immortal being needed to be spilt. Jesus was the perfect lamb whose blood was shed as payment for the sins of all mankind.

I want to be honest with you. I never used to appreciate that phrase "free from sin." I always kind of thought, "Lord, if I was free then you would let me sin." Some of us have given sin up a thousand times over. But when you learn how to overcome sin, you will enjoy the freedom that it brings.

Chapter 22: Communicating With God

In this chapter, I want us to look at what the Bible says in the book of I John about how you can begin to reach those who have been wounded by the sin and evil of the world. How can you save your friends and family? If you are not already convinced, there are a lot of reasons that you ought to be concerned about the spiritual lives of those around you, not just for their own good, but for yours as well.

We Know That We Have Wounded Brothers

"If any man see his brother sin a sin which is not unto death, he shall ask, and he shall give him life for them that sin not unto death. There is a sin unto death: I do not say that he shall pray for it." – 1 John 5:16

Blinding Lights

Do you believe that there are church members who are living in sin? Do you believe that there are Christians who are living in sin? They are wounded. It amazes me that when I go to visit a church member in the hospital, I see that other Christians have sent cards, letters, balloons, stuffed animals in an attempt to do everything in the world to make sure that they recover from that illness. But, when someone's spiritual life is wounded because of sin, we couldn't care less about them. Since when did someone's physical health become more important than their spiritual health?

Most people know the name Jerry Falwell. Sadly, most people despised him because of his hard stand on sin, but he said something that I thought was great. Appearing on Phil Donahue's program, he defended the faith for an hour against Hindus, Muslims, liberals and everyone in between. They showed a commercial supporting a supposed evangelical organization talking about the state of the environment and how we all ought to take care of the earth, but it never mentioned Jesus Christ. Afterward, they asked him what he thought about it, and Falwell explained that if they were really evangelicals, they ought to be out evangelizing the world instead of trying to save this old dead planet.

I don't think there's anything wrong with recycling and taking care of the world that God gave us, but we have become desensitized to the spiritual world. Yet, you can not only become desensitized to spiritual ethics and morals but also sensitized to the ethics and morals of the world. Thank God for the world he gave us, and conservatives probably don't do all they should to help preserve our environment, but we ought to care more about the spiritual world than we do about the physical world.

One of my favorite preachers is a Jamaican man named Peter Lord who said that people lie everyday and don't even know it. The way it happens is simple. We ask someone a question about their health because that's all we're concerned with. We aren't really concerned with their spirit. Still, when someone asks you how you are doing, it doesn't matter if you just found out you've got three days to live, your house just burned down and the dog ran away, you're going to look at them and say, "I'm doing just fine; how are you?" That's what we've been trained to do; but if the spirit was what it was all about, when someone asked you how you are, you ought to answer them, "I am blessed and very much so." It does not matter how bad life is for you, you are always blessed.

We have become sensitized to the morals and ethics of this world instead of the spiritual world. If it weren't for the hospitals to nurse people back

Blinding Lights

to health, there would be a lot of people dead today. Unfortunately, many people are going to face the reality of hell one day because the Christians they met day-to-day were concerned about their health but weren't concerned about their spirit.

Going beyond just those who are lost, this is vital to your family as well. I thank God for good wives, but when a husband has a cough, a wife will rush to get him some cough syrup or to get him a cough drop, but how many wives run to the aid of their husbands when he is in depression, angry, sad, hurting or frustrated. They don't seem to be in a hurry to get that spiritual medication of a Bible verse to remedy him. Women are committed to caring for their husband's body, yet often are not committed to caring for his spirit. Thank God for great husbands. If your wife is crying, you'll get her a Kleenex. If she's worried, you'll talk to her about it. But how many husbands do we have who would say, "Sweetheart, I know you are hurting right now. I don't have the words to say to make you feel better, but let's get on our knees before the Almighty. Let's pray. Why don't we talk to God about it?" You're caring for your wife's emotions but are you committed to caring for her spiritual life? As a parent, if your child gets a gash, you'll get him to the emergency room so that he will be well in his body, but when that child begins to have problems in life, do you rush him to a Christian counselor or to a pastor? You're committed to the child's body, but are you committed to his or her spirit?

So, if we all agree that we have wounded brothers and sisters on the battle field, how do we help them? John does not leave us in the dark. His simple answers to complex spiritual truths continue.

We Know That He Hears Us

"And this is the confidence that we have in him, that, if we ask any thing according to his will, he heareth us:" – 1 John 5:14

We know that we have brothers who are wounded in sin. We know that God can give them life. Now we see that we know for sure that if we pray to God, he's going to hear us. Your greatest weapon of spiritual warfare to defend your wounded brother is prayer. I know how that sounds. You've heard enough of preachers talking about the magic of prayer.

When I was in kindergarten, I wanted a girlfriend. Not just any girl--I wanted Katie. She was the only one for me. My knowledge of romance was of course limited to what I gleaned from Saturday morning cartoons, but I was determined to find a way to make her mine. I decided to draft a letter that I would send to her and win her heart.

Unfortunately, in kindergarten, writing letters is a daunting task. Thus, I enlisted my father to help me in the process. Clever as I was, it occurred to me that Katie would no more be able to read the letter than I was able to write it. Knowing this, I sent it to her mother. I'll never forget what it said; it was a literary masterpiece. "Dear Katie's Mom, Can Katie be my girlfriend? Sincerely, Braxton." Short, sweet and to the point. The next day at school, Katie walked over to my lunch table and took a bite out of my peanut butter sandwich and the romance had begun.

It didn't matter how much I wanted Katie as my girlfriend, I couldn't make her want the same thing. It didn't even matter how much my daddy wanted her to be my girlfriend, he couldn't make her want the same thing; and some of you who've got bachelor sons who are 40 years old and not married need to learn that. I knew that there would sure be a lot better chance that she would share a peanut butter sandwich with me if it came from her own mother.

Now, in that same way, if one of my friends is in sin, I cannot do anything to make him stop sinning. I can't do it. As a matter of fact, God isn't even going to make him stop sinning. But the one thing that you can do is write a letter to God asking him to do something about the condition of that person's life, and I'll guarantee you that they've got a whole lot better chance of listening if God is telling them.

I'm going to give you a perfect example of this. All of my life my mother has been one of the most cautious women you've ever met. I'll never forget the way it felt when we would leave to go anywhere. Maybe some of you are the same way. We would get out to the car, sit down, pull out of the driveway, and just as soon as Dad would put the car in drive, my mother would say, "Harold, did you turn off the coffee pot?"

He would say, "Yes, dear, it's off; I checked it twice."

"Well, I believe you but I'd feel a whole lot better if I could see it for myself." So, we'd pull back in to the driveway, mom would go in, check things out, come back, get in the car, and we'd pull out of the driveway again. As soon as dad put the car into drive, my mother would speak up, "Harold, did you check the stove?"

He'd say, "Yes, dear, I checked it twice."

She'd say, "Well, I believe you, but I'd feel better if I could see it for myself." We would pull back into the driveway and she'd go check again. After we'd go through this three more times for the washing machine, dryer and, if it's Christmas time, the lights on the tree, we'd be ready to go. That's how it's been all my life.

But one year, Ms. Betty, a long time family friend, came to stay with us. On one of our outings, we pulled out of the driveway and, as if on cue, my mother said, "Harold . . ." but, this time, Ms. Betty spoke up and said, "I checked everything, Marilyn. Don't worry."

My mother said, "Well, thank you, Betty." And that was the end of it. Dad and I looked at each other as if the sky had just fallen.

My mother knew that my father wasn't as cautious as she but felt that Ms. Betty was. In my precious mother's case, thank God she had that habit because if she hadn't, our house would have been destroyed more than once. However, there are some people in your life that you could tell them there was anthrax in their coffee and they'd drink it all the same. Those are the kind of people that you can show them that they are living in sin time and time again and they'll keep running back to it time and time again because, like it or not, your opinion just doesn't mean as much as it ought to mean.

So, you take it to God.

Still, some of you might think, "Well, wonderful. I don't ever have to witness to anyone again; all I've got to do is pray for them and God will handle it." Just keep in mind that it might be that the way that God handles the problem is by giving you the words that that person needs to hear. You have a tool to help them that is called prayer.

What does your prayer life look like? The world we inhabit is on a collision course with hell in part because it has had a lack of prayer. There are a lot of juvenile delinquents whose lives are ruined because of a lack of prayer. There are marriages dying because they haven't been prayed over enough. Do you understand the power of prayer? Are you a prayer warrior? The first step to reaching this county is to cover it in prayer.

We Know That Satan Controls This World

"And we know that we are of God, and the whole world lieth in wickedness." – 1 John 5:19

Listen, this world is controlled by the devil; we are in the lions den here. You and I both know Christians who are out there roaming around with bullets flying by, injured in sin, and we aren't doing a thing to help. I want to tell you that prayer really does work and not just for your life. If we ever really discover the power that we have in prayer, it will change not just our lives but the lives of others.

We have walked through the universe as it was formed and have seen undeniable evidence that there is a God. Roaming through the landscape of the world in which the messiah dwelt, we have seen the proof of his resurrection. Examining the claims of false prophets, we have seen the truth about the Lord; and sitting with John, we have been given the tools for living a life with Jesus. We can say that all of these things have been shown beyond a reasonable doubt. One remains. All of this has been done so that men can know God. We have arrived at this moment to take part in the most incredible and ancient activity that has ever existed. We may talk with God. Do this and be enraptured by the unimaginable brilliance of the blinding lights.

Appendix A: Summary of Apologetics for the Existence of the Christian God.

Chapter 1: The Lies Of Naturalism

From this, we can see that throughout its history those who espouse the philosophy of naturalism have used deceit to propagate its theory. Even today, the vast majority of high school and college biology textbooks discuss models such as the Miller-Urey and the Haekel experiment which have been disavowed by all credible scientists today. Piltdown man, Neanderthal man and an array of other evidences have been undermined and proven to be either misunderstood by their discoverers or forgeries. Evolution is a means to remove God from the equation and is built on lies.

Chapter 2: The Racism Of Naturalism

In its early days, evolution was blatantly racist. Certain people groups were considered to be of a lower level of evolution and thus not considered as valuable. Aborigines and Pygmies were murdered and their graves were pillaged, all in the name of sciences. Sketches of various skull silhouettes were touted around Europe and America showing that the Caucasian Angelo male was the most highly evolved and the black man's skull was just slightly more evolved than the monkeys. Even today, this filthy philosophy permea+ tes our society and causes hatred needlessly.

Chapter 3: The Fairytales Of Naturalism

Beauty And The Beast would be as appropriate a title for this philosophy as evolution. Beasts to men and frogs to princes are exactly the kind of myths set forth by these purveyors of untruth. Panspermia (the idea that seeds of life were spread across the galaxy perhaps by an alien race), multiple universes (an idea with no evidence), the eternal universe (a philosophy that defies the law of causality) and many other nonsensical fairytales show that evolutionists, not creationists, are the ones who need faith.

Chapter 4: The Answer To Naturalism

The chances of life arising from non-life is one in ten to the eighty-first power. One single living molecule contains more information than one thousand encyclopedias, each five hundred pages long. The molecules have a language system that they understand. The chances of this happening are so unbelievable that no rational thinking person could accept this based on the odds. Not only are the odds against it, but there's also the problem of irreducible complexity. Championed by Michael Behe, irreducible complexity shows that some things like an airplane couldn't have evolved by chance because all the pieces must be in place from the start, or else the thing can't function. The most convincing example of this is the flagellum within the human body which looks like something NASA designed.

Chapter 5: The Problem Of Relativism

The idea that truth and morality are relative is one of the most ridiculous ideas ever to be proposed by non-believers. If something is true, it is true no matter what. The simple math proposition of 1+1=2 is a true statement in Tennessee, California, Japan and on the moon. It was true five hundred years ago and will be true five hundred years from now. If someone tells you that truth is relative ask them, "Should I believe that's true?"

Chapter 6: The Prophecies Surrounding His Life

Perhaps the most convincing evidences for the Christian faith are the prophecies contained in the Old Testament about the coming Messiah. So exact are these prophecies that many have assumed them to have been injected into the biblical text sometime after Christ's life. Fortunately, the discovery of the Dead Sea scrolls discredited this argument when its fragments were dated as early as two hundred years prior to the time of Christ. Though some fragments date to the first century, the texts of Isaiah (found in Qumran cave 1) do not. When the scrolls are studied in light of this dating, one is overcome by the exactness with which the texts describe numerous details about Jesus' life. The more recent arguments are focused on the proper interpretation of these prophetic statements, but it is unfathomable to imagine that a skeptic could argue them all away.

Chapter 7: His Claims, Influence and Sanity

Many times when intellectuals who are not believers are converted, they will give the same reason that C.S. Lewis outlined in Mere Christianity. Christ was either a mad-man, a liar or the Son of God. When all the evidence is studied scrupulously, it is clear that he is the Son of God. If he was able to have such an impact on mankind that he is followed by millions over 2000 years after his earthly life, then there is something to be said for his influence. Modern day psychologists who have studied the teachings of Jesus and the events that happened sociologically when he spoke, agree overarchingly that he has none of the components of madness. Furthermore, his teachings have produced nothing but goodness on planet earth since the time he departed. The Crusades, Spanish inquisition and other horrific acts done in his name are obvious distortions of his message of love.

Chapter 8: His Death Burial And Resurrection

Attested to by historical record, eyewitness testimony and simple deductive reasoning is the fact that Christ died, was buried and rose again in a miraculous way. Debunking the swoon theory that Christ didn't actually die is the historical analysis of Roman polity regarding execution and torture. The extent to which victims were abused, coupled with the policy that Romans were held accountable by their government if a victim survived an execution, shows that there is no way Christ could have survived. Archaeological evidence for the entombment of Christ is not conclusive but is helpful when understood in context. Moreover, the idea that Jesus was not actually entombed is a modern belief that Easterners would find senseless because of the fact that the Jews and Romans wanted to put to an end the message and life of

Christ. Finally, his resurrection was attested to by over 500 witnesses, and the section of scripture containing this claim by Paul is accepted by even the hyper-skeptical Jesus Seminar.

Chapter 9: Eyewitness Testimonies

No other event is so saturated with eyewitness testimony than that of the resurrection. Not only the gospel writers but also 500 other eyewitnesses claim to have seen the risen Christ. Their testimony would be more than enough to convince any court of almost anything. Moreover, the way in which the gospel writers recorded the events surrounding the resurrection are indicative of honesty. Humiliating facts about the authors themselves are prevalent, such as women being given important roles in the discovery of Christ's resurrection or the slight dissimilarities actually showing that the writers were being honest--all things that people seeking fame and honor wouldn't have included. Finally, extra-biblical history has shown that all of the apostles, except perhaps for John, died martyr's deaths. People will live for a lie, even receive persecution for a lie, but no man will die for something he knows to be untrue.

Chapter 10: The Trustworthiness Of The Bible

No other ancient work is supported by so many matching manuscripts to verify authenticity. No other text has withstood public scrutiny and shown to contain no historical errors for over 2000 years; and, because of the testimony of the Dead Sea scrolls, we can be certain that our text is almost exactly the same as it was all those centuries ago with the only mentionable differences being punctuation and spelling. Moreover, the prophecies about Christ and the historical facts attested to by archaeology show the superiority of the Bible in the realm of truthfulness.

Appendix B: Alternate Introduction

Since the dawn of time there has been great controversy surrounding the subject of revealed truth. Does God reveal himself to man? If so, what means does He use? The extent to which these questions have daunted philosophers cannot be overstated. The resulting dialogue is thus the doctrine of revelation. While resolved in the minds of many and a thorn in the side of some, this subject is a mystery to all. To achieve a confident understanding of such an issue the inquirer must discover what the competing views of the doctrine are, as well as the various forms it may take. Determining the proper context of both general and special revelation, and clearly defining their terms, we may produce a clear and useable understanding of the doctrine which will be invaluable in future theological reflection.

To what extent God reveals himself to man should not be the primary focus. If there is a God, then He by nature of that title, is a supreme being, meaning that there are aspects of His being that could never be known. Thus, prior to any discussion of God's revelation, it is fitting to first explore man's capacity to know and absorb such revelation. According to R.J. Gore in his *Outline of Systematic Theology*, "We may affirm that there are two types of knowledge based on the Creator/Creature distinction" (Gore, 24). Archetypal knowledge refers to the knowledge possessed by God and is transcendent, eternal and immediate. Conversely, man possesses ectypal knowledge which is appropriate to his environment and sufficient for investigating his surroundings; yet, because it is finite, man can never know everything about God. Resulting from this is the understanding that even if God were to reveal everything about himself to man, it would not be within the scope of possibility for man to digest such information. How then can man hope to receive a message of any kind from God? There would need to be some common ground for revelation to be possible.

The means by which revelation is possible is clearly by reason. Norman Geisler, in his book, *Systematic Theology: Vol. 1,* asserts, "Since it can be shown that the basic laws of reason are based in the nature of God, they are common both to God and to finite rational creatures. Thus, a necessary condition for divine revelation has been fulfilled" (Geisler, 65). Understanding these principles, we may begin exercising his ectypal knowledge and reason in order to discover something of the truth of God. What God allows man to discover about Him through nature is then the first form of this doctrine and is referred to as *general revelation*.

General revelation is not as specific as what is studied in the Bible. However, it is necessary for a variety of reasons. James Montgomery Boice, in his book, *Foundations of the Christian Faith,* demands, "But, although such knowledge is limited, it is sufficient to remove excuse if any person fails to move on from it to seek God fully" (Boice 30). Even more boldly, Wayne Grudem demands, ". . . everything in nature proves clearly that God exists and that He is the powerful and wise creator that Scripture describes Him to be" (Grudem 143). Undeniably, general revelation has captured the interest of theologians in every century. Moreover, it is the admonition of scripture itself that man is to learn ectypal information about God through nature. Job 12:7-9 says, "Ask the animals, and they will teach you, or the birds of the air, and they will tell you; or speak to the earth and it will teach you, or let the fish of the sea inform you. Which of all these does not know that the hand of the Lord has done this." However, there are objections to the doctrine of general revelation.

A theological discussion of general revelation may begin with the much debated cosmological argument. Geisler explains, "(1)Everything that had a beginning had a cause. (2) The universe had a beginning. (3) Therefore, the universe had a cause" (Geisler 27).

This argument can be expanded into several forms, but simply put, the universe is made up of time, space and matter. Thus, the original cause of the universe must be something that is not restrained by time, does not occupy space and is not made up of matter. Such a cause could be called spiritual. The scientific "law of causality," as well as the implications of the "big bang theory," lend credence to this argument as credible ectypal knowledge about God. Yet, not everyone is convinced. In his book, *"On God and Religion,"* Bertrand Russell argues against the cosmological claims saying, "If everything must have a cause, then God must have a cause" (Russell 59-60). However, even if this rule must apply to God, God's existence as the cause of the universe at least moves the problem back one step and fits with observable science. Even the scientific laws held by atheists seem to point to God.

Moreover, general revelation shows the creative personality of God. The teleological argument is often offered as proof of God's existence. However, if the design of a thing is not enough to convince someone of a designer, then the awareness that order is sustained should. As Boice says, ". . . by the very law of averages it is quite possible that at some time all molecules of a gas or solid might be moving in the same direction instead of in random directions, and if that were the case, then the substance would cease to be as we know it and the laws of science regarding it would be inoperable" (Boice 177). Thus, the very design of the universe implies a designer, but even if it were not so the maintenance of all things would. Naturally, this shows man that God is a creative God with a knowledge and delight for beauty, and from Him mankind has inherited a desire to create beautiful things. This is just to give you a taste of what general revelation is. Simply put, it is what can be known simply by applying reason to the universe. Thus it is a vital tool we will refer to, throughout the duration of our examination.

General revelation is clearly vital to the Christian life. It allows man to be constantly reminded of God's glory. Furthermore, it gives man a platform on which to continue discovering more of God's personality as God's creation is explored. Finally, general revelation is invaluable in that it is often the only accepted apologetic dialogue believers can have with unbelievers. For this reason, believers must constantly be prepared to discuss general revelation. Before departing from this issue, it is needful to discuss another topic which is sometimes categorized as general revelation.

There exists a form of knowledge about God that is not observed in nature, nor gleaned from scripture. Whether it be called experiential, transcendental, mystical or otherwise, it is the things one may claim to know of God simply by experience and emotion. Karl Rahner, in his book, *"Foundations of Christian Faith,"* discusses this in the following way, "Even if one is not interested in mysticism and 'visions,' he cannot deny a priori that there can be a knowledge of God from and in man's individual and collective personal experience of existence" (Rahner 55). The problem with this form of revelation is that it is not objective. Man cannot confirm such ideas of God through either science or scripture. The only way of confirming such intuition is by observing it as a universal phenomenon. Thus, this sort of revelation, if it exists, is only of benefit to the recipient and not the collective work of theology. Therefore, we will not appeal to it during this study.

Unfortunately, general revelation can only take an observer so far. There are questions about God that this form of revelation simply cannot answer. Wayne Grudem gives examples, "Why did God create us? How did God make us like Himself? How can we please Him in everyday life?" (Grudem 439) Such questions may be speculated upon by observing the universe but they can never be answered objectively. In order to get such precise answers, observers would need a precise message. In short, God would have had to communicate directly and recognizably by what is called *special revelation*.

Typically, special revelation refers to what is learned about God through "Miraculous events. . . divine speech (and). . .visible manifestation" (House 22). Although each of these is categorized as special revelation, for the purpose of theology today, the primary focus will be on scripture as divine speech. This idea seems preposterous to some; however, if there is a God as general revelation indicates, and if He is personal as the moral argument implies, then it stands to reason that He would communicate with His creation. At present this is not verifiable truth, but if God desired communication with man, the most exact way to accomplish it would be through man's written language. Still, there is great confusion about which religious writings, if any, are to be viewed as divine.

When attempting to determine what is and what is not special revelation one must understand several constants. Special revelation is always, "Clear, authoritative, necessary and sufficient" (Gore 80). The inclusion of these things alone does not make something special revelation; still, their exclusion is evidence of false revelation. If these things are true, then a document claiming to be special revelation should never contradict itself or contain false information. There is only one document (or collection of documents) in history that meets these criteria and that is the Bible. For this reason, Karl Barth claimed, "The Bible is the concrete medium by which the church recalls God's revelation in the past, is called to expect revelation in the future, and is thereby challenged, empowered, and guided to proclaim" (Barth 125). Scripture itself makes the claim that it is the Word of God. In the Old Testament, there are many such verses: "And God spoke all these Words" (Exodus 20:1). "The Lord called to Moses, and spoke to him from the tent of meeting, saying. . ." (Lev. 1:1). "The word of the Lord came to Ezekiel" (Ezekiel 1:3). There are also many such verses in the New Testament: "God spoke of old to the fathers by the prophets; but in these last days he has spoken to us by his son," (Heb. 1:1,2). 2 Peter 3:16 refers to Paul's writings as scripture claiming, "…as also in all his epistles, speaking in them of these things; in which are some things hard to be understood, which they that are unlearned and unstable wrest, as they do also other scriptures, unto their own destruction." there are also many other passages that claim the divine nature of the New Testament. However, such claims about the validity of scripture are not unchallenged.

Scripture, most importantly, contains the claim that Jesus is God. However, there is religions debate about whether Christ even made such a claim. At least most "Christian" religions agree that Jesus was the greatest human to ever live. Bertrand Russell disagrees saying, "It is generally taken for granted that we should all agree that that was so. I do not myself. I think that there are a good many points upon which I agree with Christ a great deal more than the professing Christians do. I do not know that I could go with him all the way" (Russell 65). Furthermore, not only do non-theists like Russell disagree with the truth of special revelation in scripture, but some believers as well. According to H. Wayne House, David Hubbard felt that "Inerrancy is essentially irrelevant for a variety of reasons" (House 24). Clearly, if the Bible is the product of special revelation it is not accepted by all men or even all believers as such. How can the authenticity of such a book be defended?

As stated earlier, the Bible stands alone as a divine work in that it is the only collection of documents on earth that is indestructible and non-contradictory while claiming to be of holy origin. Though entire volumes have been devoted to the arguing of this case, Norman Geisler and William E. Nix summarize the evidences in their book, *"A General Introduction to the Bible,"* saying, "Such credentials are manifold, as they issue forth from the nature, unity, superiority, and universality of the Bible, as well as from archaeology, prophecy, Christian experience, and from Christ Himself" (Geisler/Nix, 124). Understanding that scripture is the primary means of special revelation today, observers must ask, "To whom is scripture a revelation?"

Is it sufficient to say that God spoke when He wrote the Bible but no longer speaks today? If that were so, it would mean that God revealed himself to man, but not to individual men. Boice claims, "What we mean when we say that the Bible is the word of God, for the full meaning of that statement is not only that God has spoken to give us the Bible but also that He continues to speak through it to individuals" (Boice 47). However, there seems to be one necessity for receiving the special revelation. Because of the spiritual nature of scripture, there is reasonably a need for a spiritual translator. Scripture seems to indicate the need for the Holy Spirit in order to understand the Bible saying, "And the Spirit is the witness, because the Spirit is truth" (1 Jn. 5:7). Thus, all that is needed to receive the special revelation of the Word of God is the Holy Spirit and the Bible itself. John Calvin certainly believed this. In his book on Calvin's life, John H. Leith explains, "The human need for knowledge of the Christian life is met, according to Calvin, by the revelation of God in Jesus Christ, in the law, and in the Bible" (Leith 45). Though there are differences in the terminology, the understanding is the same. There is a need for knowledge of Christ (which scripturally is taught by the Spirit) as well as the Bible, in order to receive special revelation. This explains how man receives revelation today. But how was revelation received during the construction of the Bible?

From the very beginning, there was spoken revelation in that God spoke to Adam. Moreover, God actually penned the Decalogue with his hand for Moses. He revealed himself in a column of fire and spoke out of the clouds at the baptism of Christ. Jesus' earthly presence was an act of special revelation as God entered the human experience directly. All of this was special revelation.

Still, understanding the basic implications of general and special revelation, what connections are there between these divisions? General revelation and special revelation enrich and inform each other. It is fascinating to see the way in which the things revealed about God in special revelation fit so well with what science observes of the universe. Even in the most recent years, when man is able to peer deeper and deeper into the universe, the Bible has not become irrelevant or incorrect. Each new scientific breakthrough seems to support the claims of special revelation. Although it is often denied, the laws of science seem to reflect the biblical discussion of God more appropriately than do the atheistic alternatives. For this reason, special revelation supports general revelation. Conversely, the opposite is also true.

General revelation enriches and informs special revelation. Clearly, many believers rule out the usefulness of general revelation by appealing to the Bible as absolute authority on all things. But there have been cases in which general revelation informed man's understanding of scripture. In centuries past, the scriptural declaration about the four corners of the earth led some to believe that the earth actually had four corners and was flat. If one took the Bible to be absolutely literal in everyway, this theory would be sound. However, as science led man to see that the earth is a sphere, it became apparent (not that the Bible was wrong) but that the phrase was a figure of speech. Moreover, in the book of Joshua, the Bible claims that the sun stood still. For this reason, many developed the understanding that the sun was orbiting the earth and the earth was the center of the universe. So strong was this belief that some individuals were even put to death as heretics for suggesting that this was not so. Once again, the Bible wasn't incorrect; it was simply speaking to the original hearers in terminology that they could comprehend. For this reason, it is clear that general revelation certainly enriches and informs man's view of special revelation.

It is no accident that man was placed in a position that he can perfectly observe the universe and study it. Moreover, the God who created that universe intended to speak directly to his creation. Reason is the platform on which these discoveries can be made. Because of this, it is clear that both general and special revelation are necessary to have a balanced view of God.

Man will never have a comprehensive understanding of God. This is not because God is cruel and will not reveal himself completely. Even if God were to completely reveal himself, man would never be able to comprehend the archetypal information that exists about God. Rather, in an ectypal way, man can know God practically. This can be done by examining the things observable in the universe that reveal the attributes of God, combined with the exact and specific revelation that comes through God's written word. Each of these veins of revelation is vital to the Christian experience and illuminates mankind's knowledge of the creator.

Barth, Karl . *The Doctrine of the Word of God Vol. 1 part 1., T & T Clark,*

Edinburg Great Britain

Boice, James Montgomery. *Foundations of the Christian Faith.* **Intervarsity press**

Geisler, Norman L. *Systematic Theology Vol 1.* **Bethany House Publishers**

Geisler, Norman L. , and Nix, William E. *A General Introduction to the Bible.* **Moody Press**

Gore, R.J. *Outline of Systematic Theology.* **Unpublished**

Grudem, Wayne . *Systematic Theology.* **Inter-varsity press**

House, H. Wayne . *Charts of Christian Theology & Doctrine.* **Zondervan**

Kung, Hans . *Theology for the third Millenium.* **Doubleday**

Leith, John H. . *John Calvin's Doctrine of the Christian Life.* **Westminster/John Knox press**

Rahner, Karl. *Foundations of the Christian Faith.* **The Seabury press**

Russell, Bertrand . *On God and Religion.* **Prometheus books**

Appendix C: The Three Wise Men

It has often been said that people who believe in some sort of unseen God are ignorant of the facts and foolish. I find this interesting since our scripture says that people who deny his existence are fools. Nevertheless, it is needful to say something about the number of brilliant individuals today who accept a belief in God as the only logical explanation for the way things are in the world. Universities often point out that only a small percentage of scientists and doctors believe in the existence of an Almighty God. I guess that's true if you consider 40%-60% a small number. Many, and perhaps most, of the more knowledgeable and learned people in the world accept the reality of God. Indeed 95% of the American population believes in him. Let no man convince you that if you believe in God you are in the minority. Having said this, I would like to draw your attention to three men that stand out even among the most brilliant individuals of the past hundred years.

EINSTEIN

Albert Einstein is respected as perhaps the smartest man who ever lived. There is not a scientist, mathematician or doctor alive who would question the brilliance of this great man. Often when a child displays great intellectual prowess in school, he is referred to as a young Einstein. Awards are given out to great achievers in Einstein's name, and when someone displays great lack of knowledge we laughingly say, "Well, he's no Einstein." Where did this reputation come from?

Einstein made two of the greatest breakthroughs in modern science by establishing two theories that have only grown stronger as history has rolled on. First is the theory of *special relativity*. Einstein argued that time is relative to where someone is and how fast they are moving. In other words, you have a time that is relative to you and I have a time that is relative to me. To explain this, you must imagine that a train passes by you at 100 miles per hour. Now, imagine that you were moving alongside the train in a car at 50 miles per hour. The train should now appear to you to be moving only half as fast as it really is because you must subtract the speed you are going from that of the train. Understanding this simple principle, we should witness the same thing with the speed of light. That is to say, if light is traveling at a particular speed, as we know that it does, then if you were in a space shuttle moving at half the speed of light, you should experience the same occurrence as with the train. But for some reason you don't. When this happens, no matter how fast we are moving, light still measures the same speed. There is only one answer to this, and it is that time for the person traveling at half the speed of light has begun to slow down. Sound like science fiction? It's not. It has been tested in a variety of ways, not the least of which was when one atomic clock was placed on a space shuttle for a trip into space and another was left on earth. When they were checked later, the time that had elapsed for each clock was different by a very, very small amount. Still, it lends credence to Einstein's theory of special relativity that time is relative to where a person is and what they are doing. A similar line of reasoning involving gravity instead of time was Einstein's other great discovery--the theory of general relativity.

Not only do the above arguments support the idea that God exists outside of time, but they are important in establishing for all readers that Einstein was a brilliant scientist and mathematician. So, what difference does it make? The fact is, Einstein believed in God. When discussing the possibility that the universe interacts with itself by pure randomness, Einstein made the great statement, "God does not play dice!" Still many have endeavored to show that he did not believe in a deity. However, consider the words of Gerald Schroeder in his book *The Science of God:* "My wife, the author Barbara Sofer, was privy to the notes of a private meeting held at Princeton between the late prime minister of Israel David Ben-Gurion and Albert Einstein. Their Conversation might have turned toward the politics of the young State of Israel. Instead, immediately they focused on what really intrigued them, whether there was evidence for a higher force directing the universe. Both agreed that there was such a force. . ." What does this have to say for us?

If you are going to argue that a belief in God requires one to be less intelligent than the average person, you are saying that about Einstein.

Hawking

The darling of science fiction fans everywhere, Stephen Hawking, is on the forefront of scientific discovery. As a theoretical physicist, Hawking has pushed the envelope in the realm of modern-day science. He has correctly predicted several major technological advancements over the past twenty years and discussed outlandish ideas such as time-travel and nanotechnology in such a way that most scientists are now taking those fields seriously. In case he sounds too far out for you, perhaps you will be interested to know that he holds the distinguished chair of science that Sir Isaac Newton once held.

Hawking has an interesting past that would be worth your time to study, but for our purposes he should be understood as one of the most intelligent men of the past 100 years. Hawking's book, "A Brief History of Time," has been more widely accepted than any other work of science in history. It remained on the bestseller list long enough that one copy was sold for every 750 people in America. Some doubt his theories, but hardly anyone dares challenge him.

His great work involves a search for an all-inclusive theory of the universe. In other words, a simple statement for how everything works. The problem with special and general relativity proposed by Einstein is that they seem to conflict with each other while both being testable and true. Thus, Hawking seeks to find the bridge between these two theories and understand with completeness the mystery of the universe. Whether or not you believe this is possible should not hinder your admiration for a man with a great enough intellect to begin such an endeavor.

The way he describes the universe is elegant and beautiful. When reading his works, you will develop a new admiration for the greatness of what

God did when he created. Far from being a writer of Christian works, Hawking says many things that most Christians would find heretical. Still, the truth of it is that Stephen Hawking believes in God. Midway through "A Brief History of Time," the reader will discover that Hawking cannot imagine the grand complexity of the cosmos outside of a creator. He often speaks of the way the creator knitted the fabric of the universe, and the design of the galaxies. The conclusion is simple--if you assert that believers in God are ignorant, then you are saying that about Stephen Hawking.

COLLINS

Francis Collins is probably the most respected and admired scientist of our day. Some have said he is the most intelligent man of our time. As a young man he ended up studying genetics by default because there just wasn't anything else as interesting. Growing up on a farm, he often marveled at the way different animals turned out from generation to generation. Because of this, he sought to discover how it all worked. As he climbed the latter of the scientific tower, he found himself in the midst of one of the greatest endeavors in the history of man, the "Human Genome Project."

The genome is the collection of genes that make up a particular species. The pig genome is the arrangement of genes that constitutes pigs, the cat genome is the arrangement of genes that makes up cats, and so on. The human genome is the arrangement of genes that constitutes human beings. Each gene in you carries information for something particular. There is information for hair, eye color, skin tone and hundreds of other attributes. Many genetic disorders occur because of problems in the world of genetics. Thus, the Human Genome Project led by Francis Collins, sought to make an exhaustive map of the human genome, establishing what each gene's function is, so that problems could be fixed. Finding just one of these genes is as difficult as finding a single burned out light bulb in a single house in a single city in the United States. As you can imagine, this took the most brilliant scientists working every day for years. The project began in the early 1980s and has just been completed. Contributing to humanity in an unfathomable way, Francis Collins and his team have brought hope to the lives of millions afflicted with genetic disorders.

Certainly, there are many ethical questions that surround the mapping of the human genome. With this knowledge, doctors could manipulate genes to create what have been called "designer babies" for which parents could decide what color hair and eyes a child might have, or how tall a child would be. Naturally, there are some big questions that must be answered ethically and certainly there are dangers involved. Still, the ultimate good in this endeavor outweighs the bad. Cures will be found, lives will be saved and humanity will be ever grateful to Collins.

Collins is a born again Christian. He came to faith while studying the works of C.S. Lewis and his moral argument. It is noteworthy to add that Collins was only convinced by Lewis after he had seen the great complexity and design involved in the human genome. Speaking in churches across America, Collins pushes his book, "The Language of God," which describes the human genome as nothing less than the title indicates. Once again, this man is arguably the most intellectually superior human being alive today, and to say that Christians are ignorant of the facts is to say that of Francis Collins.

Three brilliant men are mentioned here as evidence that the most powerful minds of the day have cast their lots with God. Those who oppose the idea of his existence must wrestle not only with the logic and facts but also with the reputation of the most unusually gifted humans at the top of the intellectual food chain.

The above-mentioned men represent the greatest minds of the past century. However, there are numerous scientists throughout history who were anything but atheist. Here is a list of quotes from those great men:

"Every one who is seriously involved in the pursuit of science becomes convinced that a spirit is manifest in the laws of the universe - a spirit vastly superior to that of man, and one in the face of which we with our modest powers must feel humble. In this way the pursuit of science leads to a religious feeling of a special sort, which is indeed quite different from the religiosity of someone more naive."–*Albert Einstein (1879-1955), theoretical physicist, scientific genius*

"There are more sure marks of authenticity in the Bible than in any profane history."–*Sir Isaac Newton (1642-1727), English physicist, one of the greatest scientists of all time.*

"All human discoveries seem to be made only for the purpose of confirming more and more the truths contained in the Sacred Scriptures."–*Sir William Herschel (1738-1822), English astronomer, he made numerous discoveries about the laws of the heavens.*

"I do not feel obliged to believe that the same God who has endowed us with sense, reason, and intellect has intended us to forgo their use."–*Galileo Galilei (1564-1642), astronomer, mathematician, physicist, he constructed the first astronomical telescope*

"The glacier was God's great plough . . . set at work ages ago to grind, furrow, and knead over, as it were, the surface of the earth."–*Louis Agassiz (1807-1873) Swiss-born U.S. naturalist, geologist, teacher*

"Never think that God's delays are God's denials. Hold on; hold fast; hold out. Patience is genius."–*George-Louis Leclerc de Buffon (1707-1788) French naturalist*

"Time was invented by the Almighty God in order to give ideas a chance."–*Nicholas Butler (1862-1947) U.S. educator*

"Nature is an unlimited broadcasting station, through which God speaks to us every hour, if we only will tune in."–*George Washington Carver (1864-1903) U.S. chemist, educator*

"The divine spark leaps from the finger of God to the finger of Adam, whether it takes ultimate shape in a law of physics or a law of the land, a poem or a policy, a sonata or a mechanical computer."–*Alfred Whitney Griswold (1906-1963) U.S. educator, historian*

"If we find the answer [the unified theory], it would be the ultimate triumph of human reason - for we would know the mind of God."–*Stephen Hawking (1942-) British physicist*

"Every formula which expresses a law of nature is a hymn of praise to God."–*Maria Mitchell (1818-1889) U.S. astronomer, educator*

"I give myself over to my rapture. I tremble; my blood leaps. God has waited 6000 years for a looker-on to his work."–*Johannes Kepler (1571-1630) German astronomer*

"Every scientific truth goes through three states: first, people say it conflicts with the Bible; next, they say it has been discovered before, lastly, then they say they always believed it."–*Louis Agassiz (1807-1873) Swiss-born U.S. naturalist, geologist, teacher*

---

[1]Schroeder, Gerald L. ***The Science of God.*** The Free Press.

[2]***Blank, Wayne. Scientists Believe In God. www.keyway.ca***

Appendix D: The Trinity-Not a Deal Breaker

Skeptics today scour the Bible and the circumstances surrounding it to find problems historically, scientifically and philosophically. They are searching for kinks in the chain, a place where Christians have dropped the ball. Amazingly, one of the strengths of our faith is that this is incredibly daunting for the doubters. However, there are a couple of issues in the realm of philosophy that are consistently held up as incontrovertible proof that Christianity is mythical in nature. One of these is the Holy Trinity.

How can three be one? Each member of the Godhead is discussed as being separate and individual in terms of personality and nature, yet all are discussed as being fully God. In fact, one of the problems of Christianity today is that we tend to think of Christ as being less than God and the Spirit being less than Christ. Actually, the

Holy Spirit is no less God than God is God and Christ is no less either. However, the purpose of this discussion is not Christianity's confusion about the Trinity, but the objections of the skeptics. There are two primary explanations for this that have been upheld by believers for years, and a third that I have developed from my own studies and reflection.

ANSWER 1:

The first explanation of the logic of the trinity is as follows. The Father, the Son and the Holy Spirit are all one individual--God with one individual personality; He simply wears different hats in different circumstances. Just as a man can be a husband to his wife, a son to his father and a father to his children all at the same time, God can be Father, Son and Holy Spirit while retaining a single personality.

This seems rational. It answers the problem of the triune God and even wraps the whole thing up in a warm picture of the family man. The problem is, at closer observation, it ends up creating more questions than it answers.

At Jesus baptism, all three members of the trinity were present and separate. Jesus was being baptized. The Holy Spirit descended upon Him, and God spoke out of heaven and literally had a dialogue with Jesus. I can understand a man being a father, son and husband simultaneously, but when was the last time you saw him be all of those things in three different geographic locations at the same time? This answer doesn't really work for me.

ANSWER 2:

The second explanation goes about the problem in a different way. Imagine that a mass of clay is lying on a table and an artist begins to form three different characters out of the clay without ever dividing the clay. In this manner a mass of clay has three forms coming out of it, but they are all connected at the bottom by the mass. You can see the idea. At no time are the Father, Son or Spirit separate from one another, but they are separate in form.

This argument takes us a step further in terms of logic, but has still not handled two problematic issues. In the metaphor, all three members of the trinity are really not separate personalities any more than my arm is a separate personality than the rest of my body. Second, it does not handle the biblical understanding of the separate nature of the Godhead. In other words, Jesus' man/God hybrid nature makes Him different entirely from God in terms of being. They couldn't be the same clump of clay.

My Answer:

As discussed in chapter three, the universe is made up of time, space and matter and had a beginning a finite time ago. We know this from the observable expansion of the universe documented first of all by the Hubble telescope, and now, countless telescopes. Because of the scientific Law of Causality, it must be concluded that something caused the universe to exist, and that cause was something not made of time, space or matter, because something cannot cause itself. Thus, we know something we may rightly call spiritual caused the universe of time, space and matter to exist. What does this have to say about the trinity?

Nothing within the created order can be used to define God. This is why there is certain archetypal knowledge about God that we may never know in this world. God stands outside of the created order. He is no more a part of it than a painter is a part of his painting. Notice this; the laws of mathematics are part of the created order. They are the glue that God used to sustain and define time, space and matter. Since they are a part of the created order, they cannot apply to God. Thus, the trinity may defy the laws of this universe without being illogical in the least. If math has nothing to say about God and his nature because they are confined to the created order, then to say that there are three in one is to muddy the nature of God. The benefit of this argument is that it doesn't try to fit God into our understanding, but it does answer the problem logically. With this perspective, we may have faith in the triune God, but it is blind faith by no stretch of the imagination. It makes sense, as God always does.

LaVergne, TN USA
23 March 2011
221194LV00001B/2/P